THE GOOGLE WAY

The Google Way

How One Company Is Revolutionizing Management As We Know It

by
Bernard Girard

no starch
press

13 12 11 10 09   1 2 3 4 5 6 7 8 9

ISBN-10: 1-59327-184-0
ISBN-13: 978-1-59327-184-8

Publisher: William Pollock
Translator: Eldon Brown
Production Editor: Megan Dunchak
Cover Design: Octopod Studios
Developmental Editor: William Pollock
Copyeditor: LeeAnn Pickrell
Compositor: Riley Hoffman
Proofreader: Gabriella West
Indexer: Karin Arrigoni

For information on book distributors or translations, please contact No Starch Press, Inc. directly:

No Starch Press, Inc.
555 De Haro Street, Suite 250, San Francisco, CA 94107
phone: 415.863.9900; fax: 415.863.9950; info@nostarch.com; www.nostarch.com

Library of Congress Cataloging-in-Publication Data:

Girard, Bernard.
  [Le modèle Google, une révolution du management. English]
  The Google way : how one company is revolutionizing management as we know it / Bernard Girard.
    p. cm.
  Includes index.
  ISBN-13: 978-1-59327-184-8
  ISBN-10: 1-59327-184-0
  1. Google (Firm)--Management. 2. Internet industry--United States--Management. 3. Web search engines--United States--Management. I. Title.
  HD9696.8.U64G66513 2009
  658.4'012--dc22
                              2008054604

CONTENTS

III
Put Users First; the Rest Will Follow

IV
Challenges and Risks

ACKNOWLEDGMENTS

First, I would like to thank all those who contributed to this book's ideas and preparation. The sources that underlie it are numerous and include conversations with current and former Googlers, bloggers, technologists, economists, and many others whose articles and papers were of great help. But I would especially like to thank all those with whom I had, in both Europe and America, the rare opportunity to discuss Google's management and methods.

Of those who helped me directly, thanks to Malo Girod de l'Ain, my French publisher, who offered me some very good advice while I was drafting this book and gave me the opportunity to test out many of my ideas on the blog he launched as soon as he decided to publish this book. Eldon Brown did a beautiful job translating the French original into English. And Bill Pollock, my American editor—I never thought someone could read a manuscript so carefully and with so deep a knowledge of the topic. He made invaluable suggestions. Working with him was a pleasure.

Finally, I would like to thank those who built Google, the wonderful search engine that gives everyone access to all the world's knowledge.

Bernard Girard
Paris, France
March 2009

INTRODUCTION:
A MANAGEMENT BREAKTHROUGH

Beginning shortly after World War I, Ford and General Motors created the large modern corporation, with its financial and statistical controls, mass production, standardization, scientifically organized assembly lines, and autonomous divisions. By the 1960s, mass distribution had created the consumer society, with its system of credit sales, self-service stores, media networks, mass media ad campaigns, brands, and international products.

In the 1980s, the Toyota Motor Corporation was the archetype of an industrial company focused on product quality combined with a corporate culture of continuous refinement. Today, Google is the company that is reinventing management methods: the way people work, how organizations are controlled, and how people are managed.

Google operates within the specialized context of the Internet economy of distributed intelligence, born in the early 1990s in Silicon Valley, California. Although the Silicon Valley environment imbues Google with an aura of carefree dynamism unlike companies such as General Motors, Ford, and Toyota, the massages, swimming pools, volleyball courts, and free lunches don't make Larry Page and Sergey Brin, Google's co-founders, any less formidable than Henry Ford or Taiichi Ohno, the creator of Toyota's lean production system.

Google can be seen as a new enterprise archetype because its management has made several innovations in human resources, production, customer relations, and most of all, control of its production operations. Google's ways are the result of its own initiatives, but Google also borrows from other technology companies, and the company collaborates (whether directly or indirectly) with the co-founders' alma mater, Stanford University. Where possible, I discuss these affiliations, but the most important thing to note is that Google first implemented these methods systematically. The company's rapid growth, the co-founders' personalities, their vision, their scientific culture, their obsessions, and the expertise surrounding them have all contributed to the construction of this unique business model that is the Google way.

My goal with this book is to provide you with the keys to understanding how and why the Google way has been successful. Although the book focuses on Google, I will also touch on companies like Amazon.com that have adopted this progressive management style.

Following an overview of Google's early days, Part I analyzes the economic model built by Google's leaders.

Part II, the largest section of the book, discusses in detail the management methods adopted by the Google co-founders—methods that are far removed from the best practices taught at the top business schools. Each area of innovation—whether in human resources, organization, development, or production—is compared to the norm and the differences discussed.

Part III continues with an analysis of the business environment that surrounded Google's development. Google's success in attracting users and in besting the competition has been largely due to its focus and understanding of its user communities. You will see how the automation of commerce, eCommerce, has profoundly changed business relationships with users by, for the first time, giving them an important role to play in a major corporation's growth. Google's obsession with putting users first has greatly contributed to the company's growth and success, and its breakthroughs in management are also breakthroughs in customer relations.

In Part IV, I speculate about the limits of the Google way and discuss the challenges that Google will face as it continues to grow. Finally, in the book's last chapter, I attempt to analyze the impact of the current global recession on Google's model.

Google's management innovations are made all the more interesting because the company is the first to have built a management model for the knowledge economy. I hope that in reading this book you will gain a better understanding of the new paradigm that is the Google way, and that, as you begin to understand it, you will find ways to adapt the Google way to your own professional environment.

PART I

An Unorthodox Corporate Saga

Google's story has been retold many times: the saga of Larry Page and Sergey Brin, two students who began their collaboration at Stanford University in the spring of 1995 with a project to improve search engine results. Today, little more than a decade later, they head one of the most successful enterprises in history.

In many respects, their story resembles that of all entrepreneurs—Steve Jobs or Bill Gates in consumer computing, even Henry Ford or Alfred P. Sloan in automobiles. But more so than most of their predecessors, Page and Brin's chosen marketplace and the context of their venture are central elements of the Google story.

1

Google co-founders Larry Page and Sergey Brin have undeniable talent. Who else in recent memory has been able to start and build a world-changing, international powerhouse seemingly overnight?

Page and Brin have the self-confidence and conviction of visionaries for whom making a fortune is not enough. They want to change the world, and they are driven by a shared desire to improve Internet searching.

Nonconformists, they make decisions that buck conventional wisdom with ease. Anyone tracking the Google IPO learned this early when Google adopted a Dutch auction format that gave the investment world quite a stir in its attempt to democratize the sale of shares.

And Page and Brin are true friends, a characteristic shared by several company co-founders before them, like college buddies Bill Gates and Paul Allen, the two Microsoft co-founders, and college friends Dan Bricklin and Bob Frankston of VisiCalc (the first spreadsheet). Steve Wozniak and Steve Jobs met as 18-year-olds at a summer IT class hosted by Hewlett-Packard. Hewlett-Packard, in turn, was founded by college friends Bill Hewlett and Dave Packard. And the list goes on.

Friendship creates a safe space for people to exchange and test their ideas, and friends can drive each other to succeed. In an environment as risky and turbulent as Silicon Valley, friendships can foster an us-against-them mentality that helps companies resist the pressures that threaten their independence.

Finally, but no less important, Page and Brin figured out how to take advantage of every available resource. In his pivotal book *Art Worlds*, the sociologist Howard S. Becker demonstrates that artists—the most individualistic of individualists—need what he terms "art worlds" to create their work. Entrepreneurs are no different. The co-founders of Google benefited from both a favorable environment and fortunate circumstances. The university they both attended, Stanford, competes with the University of California, Berkeley, to train some of the most highly skilled developers of web technology. (Two earlier large search engines, Yahoo! and Excite, also got their start at Stanford.)

Page and Brin founded Google when startup funding was available within their financial environment, and the legal environment facilitated the mobility of expertise and free circulation of ideas. Maturing hardware technologies meant that the memory and microprocessors they needed to build their engine were getting cheaper all the time, thanks to manufacturing in southeast Asia.

Direct Heirs of Artificial Intelligence

As Stanford students, Larry Page and Sergey Brin inherited a long, rich technological tradition. Using the term *tradition* in conjunction with a company that developed a brand-new technology might seem strange, but their breakthrough was a direct outgrowth of the concept of artificial intelligence (AI), which had been in development at some universities for half a century. When Page and Brin explain Google's mission, "to organize the world's information and make it universally accessible and useful," they are simply repeating the *memex agenda*—a theoretical project envisioned by Vannevar Bush, one of the more important American scientists during the presidencies of Franklin Roosevelt and Harry Truman.

Seeing the debt Google owes Bush is easy when you read an article he wrote in 1945, against the backdrop of World War II, when he was a scientific advisor to the White House:

> There is a growing mountain of research. But there is increased evidence that we are being bogged down today as specialization extends. The investigator is staggered by the findings and conclusions of thousands of other workers— conclusions which he cannot find time to grasp, much less to remember, as they appear. Yet specialization becomes increasingly necessary for progress, and the effort to bridge between disciplines is correspondingly superficial. Professionally our methods of transmitting and reviewing the results of research are generations old and by now are totally inadequate for their purpose. . . . The summation of human experience is being expanded at a prodigious rate, and the means we use for threading through the consequent maze to the momentarily important item is the same as was used in the days of square-rigged ships. . . . A record if it is to be useful to science, must be continuously extended, it must be stored, and above all it must be consulted.[1]

Bush went on to list some contemporary techniques likely to address this problem before describing an imaginary machine called a *memex*. It sounded like science fiction at the time, but this machine nourished the dreams of technology experts and artificial intelligence advocates for decades until it became a reality:

> Consider a future device for individual use, which is a sort of mechanized private file and library. It needs a name, and, to coin one at random, "Memex" will do. A Memex is a device in which an individual stores all his books, records, and communications, and which is mechanized so that it may be consulted with exceeding speed and flexibility. It is an enlarged intimate supplement to his memory.[2]

These early stages of modern Information Science were one source of Page and Brin's ambition and vision to make all the information in the world accessible. The Google co-founders were also given access to a considerable body of research. Universities played an important part in developing technology hubs, not only by training professionals who would go to work for the surrounding companies but also by making the work of their researchers freely accessible.

This tradition helped form Page and Brin's values and convictions. In particular, they had confidence in the capabilities of computers and the automation initiatives at the core of their corporate model.

The Invention of Page Ranking

As their thesis topic at Stanford University, Page and Brin chose the classification of search engine results from the Web. The subject may sound abstract or esoteric to some, but everyone involved in search at the time was focused on it.

Searching for information on electronic media is a field that goes back a long way, perhaps to July 1945 and the publication of Vannevar Bush's "As We May Think" in *The Atlantic Monthly*.

Gerard Salton is thought to be the father of modern search, having developed the System for the Mechanical Analysis and Retrieval of Text (SMART) Information Retrieval System at Cornell University in the 1960s. Since then, software engineers have worked with librarians and documentation specialists to develop software to quickly find scientific information stored in databases containing tens of thousands of book and articles. These efforts have followed two parallel tracks:

- Some automated the work of librarians, who index documents within a subject area, describe those documents with keywords, and then compile those keywords in a database called a *thesaurus* (not to be confused with the reference book of synonyms and antonyms). Employing these programs, the user (usually an expert) can perform complex research using *Boolean* operators (*and, or, not*, and so on).

- Others wanted to automate the process fully by having the computer compare the words of the request with those in the documents. In these programs, like LexisNexis from Mead Corporation,[*] the computer shows the user all the documents where the requested keywords appear, and the user can weight them by relevance. To prevent too many junk results in the form of irrelevant documents, the engineers created tools for sorting: The user can ask the machine to show only documents after a certain date, those where two keywords appear in proximity, or documents meeting other criteria.

The elegant simplicity of the latter approach intrigued data-processing specialists because the specialists didn't need to query databases manually. Anyone could enter keywords, thus eliminating the need to prepare and index documents. The hope was that documents could simply be digitized and stored in a database, available to be searched.

Language being what it is, however, the latter attempt to automate search has its disadvantages. For example, if you try to introduce synonyms or contextual meanings into the database, you create more volume and false positives. That's not necessarily a problem as long as the databases remain specialized within a limited field for use by professionals (like the legal documents for attorneys stored in Lexis), but using these programs for searching the Web was another matter.

---

[*] Now owned by the Dutch company Reed Elsevier.

When searching the Web, users could find plenty of documents containing the words they searched for, but there were too many irrelevant results. As the Web grew, and as more pages were assembled and indexed, search result quality deteriorated. As Page and Brin wrote in their 1998 paper titled "The Anatomy of a Large-Scale Hypertextual Web Search Engine," "'Junk results' often wash out any results that a user is interested in. In fact, as of November 1997, only one of the top four commercial search engines finds itself (returns its own search page in response to its name in the top ten results)."[3]

To counter this failing, early search engines vacillated between two solutions. Some limited the size of their databases because adding pages produced worse results. Others, like Yahoo!, took an approach based on the thesaurus concept: They created elaborate systems to categorize and rank sites based on topic. A webmaster wanting to register a site was told to specify its category with keywords. Once submitted to Yahoo!, specialists called *ontologists* would check the description's relevance.

The thesaurus method of search posed significant problems. For example, suppose you typed the word *horse* into a search box and then pressed ENTER for your results. In response, you would see various search categories, such as Zoology, Sports, Art, and so on. Visit the Zoology branch and you'd find sites about the animal that is the horse. Click the Sports track and you'd see pages about horsemanship and betting. The Art category would take you to sites on equestrian paintings. The Food section would reveal French recipes for horse meat. In Politics, you might find a rant by a British activist, complaining about a French conspiracy to eat his pet. Yahoo! employed hundreds of workers to analyze and sort web pages this way according to the thesaurus method, language by language, culture by culture. Clearly, the thesaurus method was inferior to and much more time intensive than the automated search method, but automated search was far more expensive and complex.

Dissatisfied with the current state of search, Page and Brin looked for, and discovered, a way to automatically classify pages found in a search by their relevance or rank. Of course, they were not alone in trying to find a solution to the search problem.

For example, search engines like DirectHit tried to classify sites according to their cumulative use. If someone followed a link to a site and stayed a long time, that site was considered to be more relevant than one that was infrequently and/or briefly visited. This is how Lycos and HotBot still rank sites today.

Ranking pages by cumulative use has certain advantages over former methods, but the method also has inherent flaws. For one, cumulative use is less than reliable. With today's tabbed browsers that open several pages simultaneously, a user might keep a page open for a long time without actually reading it, thus skewing the server statistics to make them at best unreliable, at worst meaningless. And it lends itself to cheating. If I want to push my site up on the search page, all I need to do is write a small robot program that goes to the site, stays for a few minutes, leaves, and then comes back again using a different proxy IP number. Catch me if you can.

Like the developers of DirectHit, Page and Brin decided that reputation was the best way to measure a site's quality and relevance. But rather than measure a site according to the number and duration of hits, they looked at the nature of scientific research and the importance of citations.

For example, to judge the quality of an author, an idea, or a concept, researchers check the number of quotations from the article in scholarly publications and then classify scientific articles by the number of times they are referred to in other articles. In the world of the Internet, links to pages are more or less the equivalent of citations. If I put a link in my text, encouraging readers to load a page on another site, chances are I consider it important or at least relevant. By counting the number of links to various pages, a search engine can classify those pages and obtain more reliable results. This forms the basis of Google's search algorithm.

But Google isn't that simple. For one thing, not all citations have the same value, nor do all links have the same importance. For example, a quote in an article written by a Nobel laureate and published in a prestigious journal has more value than, say, a student's article in some little-known school's newspaper. In the same way, links coming from pages that are cited often are given more weight by Google than those coming from pages with few incoming links.

Google added other subtleties as well, such as the distance between words when a query contains several, and a system of weighting that gives more value to links from sites with many incoming links but few outgoing links. This mechanism made it possible to improve search quality greatly without the need for human intervention.

As obvious as it may appear today, the method requires highly complex mathematics and involves the integration of several classes of problems. This is why initial support for Google came mainly from the scientific community. In fact, Google's initial success was due to a mix of programming theory and network sociology. And because of its novelty, Google qualifies as a genuine invention, which is why it interested scientific researchers and mathematicians.

This is an important detail. As you'll read in this book, through-out Google's history one of its main strengths has been its ability to maintain relationships with the academic community. The quality of these relationships stems from the personalities of the company's founders and their contacts with high-level researchers like Terry Winograd, their former college professor and now a Google consultant. But Google's work in areas of inquiry that interest researchers also enables the company to transform questions posed by its engineers into problems that mathematicians are eager to solve.

An Environment for Innovation

Entrepreneurs thrive and prosper where there are other entrepreneurs to nurture them.

And when it comes to *serial entrepreneurs*, entrepreneurs who have started company after company, California reigns supreme, with more entrepreneurs per square mile than any place on earth. And with those serial entrepreneurs comes venture capital. Seed money. One of those serial entrepreneurs, Sun founder Andy Bechtolsheim, put up Google's first seed money. Rumor has it that after talking to the Google founders for only a few hours, he wrote them a check for $100,000—but they couldn't deposit it immediately because they hadn't yet filed the legal papers to establish their company.

If the story is true, Bechtolsheim did more than give Page and Brin a financial start; he lent them credibility. His buying into their project sent a message to those who know that serial entrepreneurs can spot the good ideas. Having created their own companies, serial entrepreneurs know how to judge the quality of new ventures at first glance.

When evaluating new ventures for investment, serial entrepreneurs ask questions about the company like, "Does it meet the needs of users?" and "Will the money we invest be used prudently?" and "Is the economic model viable?" Their experience helps reduce the risk of financing startups and seize real opportunities quickly.

In a 2006 study titled *Skill vs. Luck in Entrepreneurship and Venture Capital: Evidence from Serial Entrepreneurs*, Paul Gompers and colleagues at Harvard University calculated that "entrepreneurs who succeeded in a prior venture (i.e., started a company that went public) have a 30% chance of succeeding in their next venture. By contrast, first-time entrepreneurs have only an 18% chance of succeeding and entrepreneurs who previously failed have a 20% chance of succeeding."[4] In a market fraught with high risk, this sort of expertise is invaluable.

California also offers young entrepreneurs a dense network of venture capital firms making deals. For example, according to a 2007 Entrepreneur.com ranking of the top 100 early-stage venture capital firms in the United States by deals made (*http://www.entrepreneur.com/vc100/stage/early.html*), about half of the top 100 firms are in California. Massachusetts is a distant second with about 25 percent of the total.

This concentration of venture capital firms makes finding technology funding in Mountain View, California, a lot easier than it might be to land capital in Sedona, Arizona, or southern Italy.

Job Mobility and the Exchange of Ideas

Serial entrepreneurs and venture capitalists obviously didn't appear out of nowhere. One reason they are more numerous in California is that the legal environment lends itself to the creation of innovative companies. Stanford professor Ronald J. Gilson, an expert on Japan and venture capital, discusses this in an article. In 1996, he analyzed the contrasting destinies of Silicon Valley and Route 128, the technology corridor near Boston. There, in the early 1980s, prestigious universities like MIT spawned most of the great names in technology, including Wang and DIGITAL.[5] But the climate soon changed.

One of the main reasons Silicon Valley flourished while its eastern counterpart stagnated was that California law prohibits restrictive noncompete clauses in employment contracts. California companies can require that employees sign a nondisclosure agreement, stating they will not exploit the company's confidential information, but such an agreement doesn't prevent anyone from going to work for a competitor. So engineers who come up with a bright idea that doesn't interest the company they're currently working for can take it elsewhere or start their own venture.

In most other jurisdictions, a new employee can be required to sign a contract agreeing not to use any knowledge gained on the job in case he or she ever goes to work for a competitor. In the case of a direct competitor, reusing that gained knowledge is often seen as inevitable, so an engineer who receives a job offer from a competing firm can be legally prevented from accepting it.

In California, the absence of noncompete clauses thus contributes to the mobility of people, ideas, and expertise. It supports the cross-fertilization of innovations and helps new ideas move from the laboratory into real-world development. It also contributes, perhaps importantly, to the quality of human resources available in the Valley. Finally, an ever-growing number of employees aren't required to change fields when they change companies. Communities of professional acquaintances can develop to exchange ideas, advice, and information about projects. All this leads to increased specialization, because people who change jobs can continue to work in the same niche and increase their expertise.

When we think about the influence of human capital on the development of technology centers, universities are usually seen as key. Their role is fundamental, of course, but the labor market's operation is also a factor. If the market supports mobility and specialization, as it does in California, the quality of available expertise improves. In 2000, at the peak of the Internet bubble, three times more teaching jobs were open in data processing at Stanford than there were candidates to fill them. All the people who could have filled the extra jobs were working in the industry. Some experts at the time warned that if the trend continued, one of California's strong suits would be threatened—but that didn't occur. By encouraging practical, hands-on learning, job mobility compensated for education.

A Short Leash

Silicon Valley's rich environment of universities, serial entrepreneurs, and venture capitalists makes it a wellspring of technological innovation. But relationships among joint-risk stock companies and entrepreneurs are seldom love affairs, and company founders are often kept on a short leash. Horror stories abound of the predatory nature of "vulture capitalists," who neglect the interests of their startup clients in favor of delivering returns to investors.

Venture capitalists often contribute their experience and expertise to the companies they finance. As part owners, many actively participate in the day-to-day management of the companies they invest in, contributing to strategic position, human resource policies, organizational structure, product development, and so on.

Many venture capitalists encourage the companies they invest in to *specialize*—to concentrate their resources in a single core activity that (they hope) will support growth (though that specialization also makes companies more vulnerable to market fluctuations).

Venture capitalists favor business activities that promise the highest returns because they are investing, after all. For example, in the life sciences, venture capitalists tend to back the development of drugs with huge potential markets over those used to treat rare diseases. They're wary of business portfolios that contain many licenses that, although they may require less total investment, will bring in less projected income.

Venture capitalists also tend to press companies to patent their inventions in order to increase their intellectual property value and, hence, their commercial value. Patenting protects products in an industry that has high employment turnover, and even if the company disappears, its patents will still have some commercial value.

Patenting and specialization may work for the life sciences, but when it comes to technology, this strategy has its disadvantages. For one, over the long term, patenting threatens to slow the movement and sharing of ideas that have allowed the technology business to develop so quickly. In the IT industry, technology spillovers have occurred frequently because intellectual property was poorly protected. In fact, until the late 1990s, technology companies rarely filed patent applications for software because companies assumed the patent applications would automatically be rejected. The algorithms at the heart of software or that define elements such as interfaces are like mathematical formulas, which cannot be protected.

Code is protected by copyright law as speech, but accomplishing the same functions in a particular piece of code by writing similar code, without actually copying and infringing the original program, is relatively easy.

Things changed in 1999 when Amazon.com was granted a patent for "A Method and System for Placing a Purchase Order Via a Communications Network," what's more commonly known as *one-click ordering*. Since then, the United States Patent and Trademark Office has doled out software patents with increasing frequency, leading industry observers like Harvard law professor Lawrence Lessig to call the situation disastrous: "This is a major change that occurred without anybody thinking through the consequences. In my view, it is the single greatest threat to innovation in cyberspace, and I'm extremely skeptical that anybody's going to get it in time."[6]

The birth of so many software patents poses a real threat to the growth of the IT industry. For better or worse, much of the IT industry's progress can be traced to the frail protection of intellectual property. For example, Microsoft's Windows interface is a copy of Apple Computer's Macintosh operating system, which in turn was copied from the Xerox Star's windowed interface.

We can probably safely assume that if data processing industrialists had been able to protect their intellectual property as well as those in the automotive or aviation industries did, personal computers would not be as ubiquitous as they are today. By the same token, had companies been granted patents for tools like spreadsheet, word processing, and database programs, we would likely have few, if any, tools to choose from when working on our personal computers.

Finally, the oversight and influence of venture capital firms on new businesses contribute to the early and, I would argue, sometimes premature professionalization of the companies they invest in as the venture capitalists define compensation policies and bring in experienced upper-level managers. Certainly, these contributions support growth, but they also promote conformity. The solutions that these experienced professionals tend to recommend are, above all, safe ones that worked at other companies.

And that's what makes the Google story so interesting. Page and Brin could not have built Google as we have come to know it if they had been subject to the heavy supervision interference of venture capitalists and the pressure to patent and specialize.

Winning Independence

To guarantee their independence, the Google founders played joint stock-holding companies against one another. After several months of negotiations and battles, they struck a deal with two venture capital firms, with each taking equal shares in Google. This odd arrangement would play a significant role in Google's future success because Google immediately doubled its network of contacts and advisors. But perhaps more importantly, this arrangement relieved the pressure Page and Brin would have encountered had they worked with only one investor who would likely have pushed for them to build a more traditional organization.

Page and Brin demonstrated their independence again at the time of Google's initial public offering (IPO). Generally, when a company goes public, it nearly always turns over the job to investment bankers who know how to skirt the rules while avoiding trouble with US Securities and Exchange Commission regulators. These same bankers also know how to enrich themselves and their cronies as a result of taking companies public.

The mechanism that the investment bankers use is relatively simple: Estimate a weak opening price for the stock by taking a survey of "selected" potential investors. That way, those who buy shares at the beginning will be able to sell their stock for a profit once the price rises.

For this mechanism to be fully effective, shares are reserved at the deflated "opening price" for friends, who then bid up the stock by trading during the first few days it is on the market. At the same time, the bankers make sure most potential investors have no access to the stock beforehand so that demand for the IPO will increase and investors will be eager to buy.

The few investment bankers who specialize in these IPO manipulations have become masters at the art of anticipation, touting stocks during road shows held for likely investors and their financial advisors. These meetings are part of the services that investment banks sell to their customers—at very high prices, of course.

Page, Brin, and Eric Schmidt (the manager they ultimately recruited at the behest of their investors) wanted nothing to do with investment bankers. Instead, they researched their options and found a system to avoid those shenanigans: an auction with sealed bids that would set the price of the stock, also called a *Dutch* or *Vickrey auction*.

In a Dutch auction, the seller sets an opening price and specifies the number of shares offered for sale. Investors bid by specifying the quantity of shares they want to buy and the price they are willing to pay. All investors whose bid is equal to or greater than the offering price pay the same final price, including those who bid higher. Investors who bid less than the final price get no stock.

The principles behind this unusual and somewhat elaborate system were originally formulated by William Vickrey, an economist who was awarded the Nobel Prize for the concept in 1996. They've since been put to use by William Hambrecht, a well-known Silicon Valley financier whose previous investment bank had contributed to the financing of companies like Apple, Genentech, and Sybase.

In 1999, Hambrecht sold his firm (Hambrecht & Quist) to Chase Manhattan Corporation. Through his new company, WR Hambrecht + Co, he began capitalizing companies with a Vickrey-inspired method he termed *OpenIPO*, a transparent allusion to open source. His first client in 1999 was a vineyard, Ravenswood Winery. Following a successful IPO, he took several more companies public using his OpenIPO system, including *Salon*, the Internet magazine.

These were fine companies, whose IPOs brought in tens of millions of dollars, but they were modest in size when compared with Google.

The remarkable feature of the OpenIPO bidding system is that it discourages auction hysteria and brings a measure of prudence to the IPO. Buyers know that the higher their bid, the better their chances of ending up with the number of shares they want. But at the same time, bidders know that they have a good chance of paying less than their offer because the ultimate IPO price precipitates the sale of all shares. In this way, OpenIPO contradicts standard auction practices, as announcing the final price a buyer is willing to pay up front is advantageous. Buyers can do so with confidence, knowing they won't pay more than necessary.

When the Google founders chose OpenIPO as their method of going public, bypassing the traditional investment bankers, they caused quite an uproar in the investment community, which complained bitterly about the perceived arrogance of Google's two young founders. The trade press was also skeptical, lambasting Page and Brin when *Playboy* magazine published an interview with the founders in the September 2004 issue—during the mandatory *quiet period*, when they were prohibited from making public statements. Even though, according to *Playboy*, the interview had been conducted on April 22, 2004 (Page and Brin announced the IPO on April 29, 2004), the publication of their interview during the quiet period amounted to an involuntary violation. Page and Brin took the heat in many news articles.

But the auction IPO and this perceived quiet period violation weren't the only things that riled the investment community. Also irksome was the fact that Page and Brin had engineered a way for top management to retain a majority of votes on most issues using a *two-tiered voting system*. This two-tiered system is commonly used in Europe but rarely seen in the United States, where only media companies use it to ensure their editorial independence. The system is based on the assumption that a brand's founders have a long-term stake in its reputation that outweighs the interests of financiers or transitory stockholders.

As a demonstration of their independence, Page published an open "Letter from the Founders" (co-signed by Brin) to potential investors, stating in part that "Google is not a conventional company. We do not intend to become one." Consequently, he wanted investors committed for the long term. "As a private company, we have concentrated on the long term, and this has served us well. As a public company, we will do the same."[7] These words are fraught with mistrust of the financial markets and dismissive of the mercenary decisions typically dictated by Wall Street. The financial community was furious.

By choosing unconventional methods, Page and Brin wanted to avoid diluting their voting power and to ensure their ability to pursue long-term objectives unencumbered and without interference. By using the OpenIPO mechanism to invite investors to name a price they considered fair, their bidding system helped attract investors who were committed to Google's best interests and its future success. Also, by making buyers rather than investment bankers the judges of a fair stock price, they effectively enhanced their company's value.

What About the Rest of Us?

People often wonder whether the Google experiment can be replicated elsewhere. That is, can it really be used as a model, or did Page and Brin just come along at the right time and understand how to take advantage of the entrepreneurial climate in Silicon Valley?

As I explore that question throughout this book, remember that Google was created largely by bucking that system. In fact, Page and Brin developed an organization with management methods that contradict most of what they were told to do by venture capitalists and other Silicon Valley professionals.

Entrepreneurs are often depicted as heroes or adventurers, more willing to take risks than the average executive. That sounds romantic, but the image is pretty far from reality. In fact, successful entrepreneurs tend to be risk averse and to take only a few, calculated risks.

In creating their company, Page and Brin took few risks. As students, they weren't leaving good jobs to venture into unknown territory, as Jeff Bezos did when he founded Amazon.com. Educated at Stanford University, a school known for nurturing entrepreneurs, in an area of the United States filled with venture capitalists and new businesses, they had little to lose if they failed.

They succeeded because they had the self-assurance to buck the trends, to not conform. If any one characteristic distinguishes Page and Brin, it is probably their desire for independence and autonomy. They are more creators than gamblers. They invented a new model of organization and management strategy that can be applied elsewhere, either in whole or in part, whether to your nascent business or a larger corporation. That process has already begun, as you'll discover in the rest of this book.

2

THE GOOGLE ECONOMIC MODEL

Like network television shows and other search engines, Google is free but with certain strings attached. For example, the "free" programs on network television are only free to view if you own a television set or a computer—and then only if you pay your electricity bill. You'll also have to watch commercials (or work to avoid them) if you still want to watch the programs for "free." In the same way, the Internet is not "free" for most people, who pay to subscribe through a service provider. Although you may not notice the cost because you get so much in return, somebody pays for everything. This reality disproves the fallacy of getting something for nothing.

Google Is Free, But . . .

After that cautionary note, let's examine some "free stuff" in economic terms. Anthropologists first explored this concept with Marcel Mauss's analysis of the *potlatch*, a Native American ceremony where a tribe hosts a festival and lavishes gifts on the guests who are then expected to reciprocate later. This practice constitutes a *gift economy*, with rituals involving exchanges of property and prestige through symbology and relationships.[1]

The Native American potlatch custom is one example of an economy based on gift exchange. More contemporary examples include *open source software*, which is free software developed by groups of dedicated but unpaid volunteers. The creators of open source software give users the source code for their program and the right to use, copy, modify, and improve it. In exchange, the creators expect users' contributions to improve the program, whether those contributions are simply comments and suggestions or actual development and testing.

Traditional scientific research is another example of a gift economy. Scientists publish their research in print journals or online and present their results at conferences. Other scientists cite their work, and the researchers become more prestigious within the scientific community as the number of citations to their work increases. The scientific community benefits from the increased pool of knowledge, and individual scientists benefit from their growing status and the awarding of more grants or funding.

One final example of gift economics might be what are known as *captive sales* techniques. Manufacturers of inkjet printers give the printers away or sell them at ridiculously low prices, knowing they will get a return later by selling ink cartridges.

Two-Sided Markets

Search engines, which finance free search results by selling advertising, use what economists call a *two-sided market* (sometimes called a *double-sided market*). All media—including television, radio, magazines, and newspapers—would be far more expensive if it weren't for advertising revenues. Other business sectors apply similar techniques: Your credit card appears to be free (or almost free) when you use it for purchases, but the merchant accepting the card pays a fee to the company that issued it and you, of course, pay interest if you carry a balance.

In every case—search engine, newspaper, or credit card—the company offers its products or services to two markets: reader and advertiser or customer and merchant. The more subscriptions or placements the company accumulates in the first market, the more services the company can sell to the second market. The more readers a newspaper has, the more ad pages it sells to advertisers. The more cardholders Visa has, the greater the number of merchants that will accept the card.

When companies adopt a two-sided market model, their challenge is to find the right balance between a price that will allow them to maximize product placements while still enabling them to sell services effectively.

Search engine companies vacillated for a long time between offering completely free services and selling low-cost subscriptions. The free service model won, largely because of the overhead that subscription transactions would have required. For example, if Internet searches had been based on paid subscriptions, users would have had to enter some sort of payment information and remember various passwords. The cost in lost users in addition to the transaction costs might actually have impeded the development of Internet search tools.

By offering their services for free, the large search engines created a climate that encouraged fast growth. An advertising market was created so companies like Yahoo! and Excite, as well as their early competitors who wanted to give their service away, could generate revenue by selling ad space at high rates.

The Cost-per-Click Advertising Model

Google found another way to generate ad revenue—the company's co-founders borrowed the cost-per-click system from Overture Services, Inc. Overture, created in 1998 under the name GoTo, offered advertisers the option to bid on how much they would be willing to pay to appear at the top of search results. Advertisers paid a fee each time someone clicked a link to their website.

Google combined this model with contextual ad display, wherein an ad appears only when a user's query matches keywords chosen by the advertiser within specified geographical areas. Google also decided to let advertisers decide how much they wanted to pay per click. Here, economists will recognize the principle of price differentiation formulated by the engineer-economist Jules Dupuit in 1849: "To set a price for a service, don't base it on what it costs the provider, but instead set the price according to the importance of the service to the user."[2]

By adopting a cost-per-click strategy, Google limited advertiser risk and reduced the uncertainty connected with all mass advertising. Essentially this change was a tweak of a detail, but it was a major breakthrough.

Google's engineers discovered one of the best kept business secrets: Advertisers generally can't evaluate the effectiveness of an ad campaign. In fact, according to a 2005 study by the Association of National Advertisers (ANA):[3]

- Seventy-three percent of managers did not know how to determine an ad campaign's effect on sales.

- Only 19 percent of managers were satisfied with their ability to measure the return on investment from advertising.

- More significantly, 63 percent could not estimate the potential impact on sales if their advertising budget was reduced by 10 percent.

Uncertainty affects all advertisers, but especially small ones who lack the resources to buy or perform market research on their ads' effectiveness. These small advertisers—individual consultants, small businesses, and specialized companies that can't afford mass media—were the ones Google attracted early on.

With traditional media such as newspapers, radio, and TV, the advertiser pays according to the size of the audience that *might* see an ad. The equivalent measure on the Internet is *cost per thousand* $(CPM)^*$ page views when an ad is displayed.

A CPM pricing strategy favors advertisers with the most money because only they can afford to pay for media with large audiences. The overall cost is high, but the cost per impression is very low. When the cost of advertising is based on audience size, for example, a 30-second commercial on CBS is less expensive per impression than a four-color, full-page ad in a magazine with only a few thousand readers.

By tying payment to a result, cost-per-click changed the rules of the game. Small-budget advertisers get less exposure than those who spend more, but they aren't entirely excluded from the medium. If they plan skillfully and create effective ads, they may do very well.

In fact, Google gives priority to ads that get the best results. Advertisers bid on keywords or phrases and set a budget for their ad campaign. Ads that are clicked more often, using the same keywords, appear higher on the page. As a result, although one advertiser may bid more than another for a particular keyword or phrase, that advertiser's ad may appear higher on the page because users click it more often. While the cost-per-click (CPC) is often higher than CPM's cost per audience member, in the world of CPC an advertiser's financial clout is less important than ad quality and its ability to attract potential customers. Because advertisers decide what they are willing to spend, even advertisers with tiny budgets can buy advertising.

This strategy has proven to be very powerful. According to Anil Kamath, chief technology officer of Efficient Frontier, Inc., a search-engine marketing firm in Mountain View, California, in 2006 Google earned about 30 percent more revenue per ad impression than Yahoo! did. (Yahoo! sold space to the highest bidder until it announced a similar bidding system in early 2007.)[4]

---

* Here *M* represents the Roman numeral for 1,000.

The Power of Minimalist Ads

Overture may have invented CPC, but Google created a new advertising paradigm by selling minimalist ads of 10 to 15 words, including the URL for the advertiser's website. Known as *AdWords*, the ads in the right column of a Google search results page look more like classified ads in a newspaper than like glitzy TV commercials. These little rectangles are unobtrusive and, in fact, nearly invisible by normal advertising standards.

Not only did Google refuse to sell any advertising on its home page, but it also relegated advertising literally to the margins. This placement avoids frustrating people who come looking for answers, so the vast majority of users who have no interest in the ads aren't exasperated. At the same time, someone who finds information about an offering that seems relevant to his or her search can get more information about it with a single click.

This choice dismayed advertising people who were used to creating ads designed to startle viewers and grab their attention. They had to find new ways of earning their living, and many did, by selling search engine optimization. Part of *search engine optimization* (*SEO*) involves determining the best keywords to use to target a particular audience in order to get the most traffic and conversions. The advice and tools developed by SEO specialists is certainly useful, but a small business owner can still write his or her own ads without paying for that advice. The ads themselves cost nothing to produce, and they can be revised at any time with a few minutes of thought.

Google's choice to offer this advertising format was another contrarian stroke of genius, though the basis for the decision probably had more to do with the founders' paradoxical aversion to publicity than it did to any economic rationale. Because they put the performance of their search engine first, they didn't want advertisements to compromise the results. At best, banners would distract users who came seeking information; at worst, users might be tricked into mistaking an ad for a search result.

Ads That Inform Rather Than Persuade

The minimalism of Google's ads offers several benefits. For one, response to the ad is direct and immediate. Users see an interesting headline and then click the ad to visit the site or buy the product. In addition, time to transaction is much shorter, and advertisers can quickly measure the performance of their campaign and the cost of sale.

Unlike persuasive ads in traditional mass media, which try to attract consumers to brands and gain their loyalty, Google ads are mostly informative. Persuasive ads usually want to change consumer habits—get them to switch from a manual razor to an electric shaver, from fabric handkerchiefs to paper tissues, from soap to gel. Informative ads, on the other hand, mainly provide product information, including features, uses, benefits, and prices. They attempt to convince consumers by appealing to reason—by providing consumers with facts that make them want to buy. Because Google ads offer very limited space (95 characters total at this writing), advertisers must attract viewers with just a few keywords: They must get right to the point.

The exclusive use of informative ads changes the rules of the game, giving advertisers without the massive financial resources often necessary to build a brand name more opportunities. Informative ads decrease the need for the incessant repetition that persuasive ads require to be effective—the assumption being that the more often an ad is seen, the more likely consumer behavior will change. In other words, the more people see a message repeated, the more likely they will be to change how they shave, their brand of detergent, or the car they drive.

With informative advertising, the story is different. Once people have the information, they will eventually make a purchase or they won't. Viewers have no reason to click again and revisit the same site. This allows an advertiser with a modest budget to run an effective ad campaign on Google.

Automating Ads Reduces Overhead, Not Confidence

For Google to have built a sales force to reach small advertisers using conventional methods of ad sales would have cost a fortune. Google could never have launched its venture by hiring salespeople to sell ads; the cost of selling the ads would have been far greater than the income from selling those ads.

AdWords succeeded because Google had the good sense to automate the ad placement process, thereby drastically reducing the cost of sales. Automation eliminates the need for sales reps; instead, customers come directly to Google. Whether large or small, experienced or inexperienced, any advertiser can construct an ad campaign without human intervention.

Of course, in order to make its automated advertising system work, Google had to gain the confidence of its surfer-merchants, many who were initially resistant to or confused by the concept. After all, trusting faceless and voiceless interactions with a company can be difficult, never mind paying via the Internet, too.

Paying via the Internet could have been an obstacle were it not for two features built into the system.

The first feature is simply the elegance of the process. Like the intuitive Macintosh GUI that makes Apple products so friendly and easy to use, the design and user-friendliness of Google's AdWords interface has helped make it a winner. Any advertiser can easily understand how ads are placed and how to place an ad by following the step-by-step directions.

The second feature is more subtle. Page and Brin understood early on that people trust machines at least as much as they trust other human beings (this confidence in computers is typical of Silicon Valley). In other parts of the United States or the world, people might have hesitated, wondering whether customers would really trust machines.

Brin and Page believed that people would trust machines, perhaps because they were familiar with the work of Joseph Weizenbaum. Weizenbaum, a founder of artificial intelligence (who later became one its harshest critics, largely because so much research was financed by the Pentagon), was one of the first to highlight the singular and strange relationship between man and machine—or rather, computer program. In the early 1950s, he designed a computer program that allowed a human being to converse with a machine. Much to his surprise, he discovered that ordinary people "become emotionally involved with the computer and . . . anthropomorphize it."[5] But even if Page and Brin hadn't read Weizenbaum, they certainly worked with researchers who had looked further into the relationship between human and machine and similarly discovered that "an individual's interactions with computers and television sets are fundamentally social and natural, just like interactions in real life."[6] Many studies have shown that the rules of reciprocity and courtesies that govern our contacts with friends are also used in our interactions with machines.

Page and Brin set out to design a computer-based system that would create a comfortable and familiar environment and, in the case of financial transactions, mimic the mechanisms people rely on to build confidence in a relationship: Specifically, a person follows a learning curve, gradually engaging as he or she gains more experience. People are prudent, starting with small risks, and they are most comfortable when they have a way to back out quickly in case of disappointment. The next section takes a meticulous look at Google's payment methods for advertising, which clearly demonstrate that programmers took human transactions as the starting point.

Competitive Bidding

When setting the payment structure for Google ads, following a model like Yahoo!'s and setting a standard cost-per-click would have been simple. Instead, using Overture's example, Google chose a bidding system. Advertisers compete for keywords, and the more they do, the higher the price of the keyword.

Instead of using traditional ascending bids, as practiced in auction houses, Google's leaders chose a system in which the bidder states the maximum price he or she is ready to pay for a keyword. This price remains confidential, known only to Google. The sale is made to the person making the highest bid, but at the next highest price. The system encourages bidders to indicate the price they are actually ready to pay because keeping it secret from the seller offers no benefit; this system also prevents collusion because bids are confidential.

The AdWords bidding system resembles the method used for the Google IPO, but the system differs in two important ways. First, bidding is continuous; the goal is to buy not a product, stock, or contract, but a position on a screen that may change constantly. This encourages advertisers to experiment, vary their list of keywords and settings, and correct their initial decision. They can, in other words, train themselves by tinkering. The gains from improvements can be significant. As early as 2004, two Australian researchers (Brendan Kitts and Benjamin Leblanc) demonstrated that modifications could multiply an ad's effectiveness by four times.[7]

The bidding mechanism may appear complex at first glance, but most of the complexity happens on the Google side. Advertisers are led through the process of setting a budget and their maximum bid price for keywords; Google performs the calculations.

By assigning advertisers higher positions based on both what they pay and the effectiveness of their ad (multiplying the payment price by the click-through rate and ranking ads according to the result), Google encourages advertisers to invest time in learning to compose effective ads, with both parties directly benefiting.

The bidding process also offers many advantages to both the customer and Google. For one, bidding eliminates rate negotiations between advertisers and salespeople as well as concerns about price increases, and it makes billing simple and more transparent. The customer decides how much to pay, and the market determines the price.

Google has seen a direct benefit from the bidding process, too. In fact, the average price of Google's ads has probably risen higher than it would have if Google had fixed its ad prices. According to advertisers interviewed by MarketWatch in 2007, keyword search prices on many terms had risen between 40 and 60 percent in 2006.[8]

Of course, bidding success requires that advertisers spend time learning the process and the rules of the game. But this time is not lost: Well-chosen keywords result in more clicks, more visitors to advertiser websites, and more revenue for Google.

No Content, No Portal

Had they taken the advice of experts, Page and Brin would have built a portal site with multiple services, just like their principal competitors. They chose to do just the opposite instead—to produce no content on their own, focusing instead on offering tools to find or produce content.

No Shortage of Content

Although Google doesn't generate its own content, the company very actively develops and purchases tools to offer individuals ways to create web-based content, whether that content is contained in a Blogger blog; an article in Knol, Google's "Wikipedia killer"; a website created with Google Sites; a video posted to YouTube; pictures displayed on Picasa; or code hosted by Google Code. And the list goes on. Thanks to these free tools, anyone can produce and publish content that attracts visitors and offers more opportunities for Google to serve up ads.

This daring, counterintuitive choice allows Google to economize by not hiring journalists, graphic designers, and web developers to build a content-based portal and to concentrate its modest resources instead on the core business, the search engine, while competitors divide their energy between search and newsroom activities.

One side benefit of Google's choice to not offer content is that it eliminates the problem that advertising-supported media face when advertisers get upset about a journalist bad-mouthing their product. The relationship between advertisers and media is a delicate one that creates conflicts between reporters who demand the freedom to criticize and publishers who are worried about losing advertising accounts. Most media deal with this conflict in the simplest way possible—by not critiquing consumer products.

Certainly, objective criticism of products has a market, as demonstrated by the popularity of customer reviews on sites like Amazon.com, news stories that expose frauds of all types, and magazines like *Consumer Reports* (which carries no advertising). Although radio and television broadcasts or newspaper columns critiquing the products bought every day would surely be successful, they would continually endanger the income of the stations or newspapers that run them.

Unlike other ad-supported media, Google doesn't owe anything to its advertisers, so it can run any ad, anywhere, whether that ad appears alongside links to sites that criticize the products or services being advertised. This means significantly lower overhead because ad placement is automated, so staffers do not need to evaluate where each ad runs. This also causes fewer headaches and maintains integrity, even though Google itself does not produce any content.

But Google's lack of original content has a risk, too. Without content or a web portal to act as home base, Google's visitors remain on the Google site only long enough to find the link they're looking for and then move on. This might be one reason that Google has diversified into other, stickier products, like Maps, Mail, and News, and offers its own web browser, Chrome, as a way to capture and keep visitors.

How to Keep Channel Surfers

Channel surfing is a natural outgrowth of the *free information* movement that encourages the curious to hop from channel to channel or from site to site. But when your core business is selling ads, how do you capture maximum revenues if you keep losing visitors? How do you get Internet surfers to return to pages with ads when you don't offer content and when the goal of your search engine is to find pages that interest searchers and send them to those pages as quickly as possible? Let's look at four strategies that characterize Google's formula for success:

Free search Google's first solution to this problem was to encourage site owners to add a free Google search engine to their pages. After all, how can anyone find what he or she is looking for on a large site without a search tool? By giving away what others had tried to sell, Google gained a massive presence on the Web that increased brand awareness and referrals to the Google home page.

AdSense A second solution was AdSense, a revenue-producing program for site owners that accounted for 30 percent of Google's ad sales revenue in 2008. AdSense crawls the content of pages and automatically delivers ads that relate to them. Each time a visitor clicks a Google ad placed on a page, the site owner receives part of the payment. As a secondary benefit, the program provides a way to remunerate site authors without infringing copyright and provides incentives to increase free content.

Free tools   A third way that Google keeps visitors is with tools designed to become a part of the web surfer's daily life. These include communication tools like Gmail and Google Talk, planning and organization tools like Google Calendar and Google Maps, productivity tools like Google Notes and Google Docs, analysis tools like Google Metrics and Google Trends, mapping tools like Google Earth and Google Sky, and so on. Each of these services is designed to exploit the potential of a search and to offer more ways to attract and keep visitors—and advertisers—within reach of Google properties.

Ubiquity   Finally, Google intends to expand its reach by being everywhere. On your cell phone or PDA (with the G1 cell phone and mobile apps), computer, and even in your car (with the GPS-connected Google Maps and handsfree voice search). By expanding the company's reach, Google stands to expand its revenue as well.

The Double Long Tail

By empowering advertisers who would otherwise have little or no access to the mass media due to their limited financial resources, Google has democratized advertising and dramatically expanded its base of ad revenue. Today, a very large part of its sales revenue comes from hundreds of thousands of advertisers who would be considered too small for traditional media to cater to.

In his work *The Long Tail*, Chris Anderson describes a "long tail" as the very long, gentle slope of a graph comparing number of receipts per user and total number of users.[9] On the graph, the long slope is shown in light gray. The farther you go along the line, the lower the amount of each sale made to each advertiser, but the greater the number of advertisers paying these small amounts. Taken in aggregate, each of those smaller advertisers adds up to a very significant whole.

By broadening search into every conceivable market and monetizing each minor search with nickel- and dime-sized ad revenue, Google capitalizes on this concept of the long tail. But that's only part of the story.

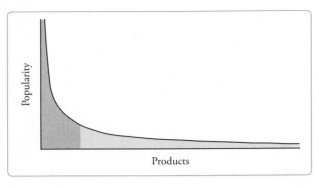

The long tail

The long tail phenomenon describes a statistical distribution called a *Power Law*, or a *Pareto distribution*, which has been described in many forms over the years. This distribution is also called the *80/20 rule* (meaning that 80 percent of a machine's malfunctions will be caused by the failures of 20 percent of its parts) as well as *Zipf's law* or *Lévy's general distribution*. In these statistical distributions, found in many variations, a small number of things (words in a language or malfunctions) occur very often, and the greatest number occur less often. If the slope is fairly long, these infrequent phenomena, in total, can represent a volume as large or larger than those that occur more frequently.

It seems clear that by lowering search costs and increasing the availability of products, the Internet could substantially increase the collective market share of niche products, thereby creating a longer tail in the distribution of sales. For example, several academic studies have since confirmed Anderson's theory while also demonstrating that the long tail applies to many products. For example, in their 2004 study, Kohli and Sah found evidence of a long tail in food and sporting goods.[10] Additionally, they found evidence that online recommendations can alter buyer behavior, which is also supported by the work of two researchers who, based on a study of Amazon.com data, concluded that "doubling the average influence of recommendations on a category is associated with an average increase in the relative demand for the least popular 20% of products by about 50%, average, and a reduction in the relative demand for the most popular 20% by about 12%."[11]

Academic research also reveals that the concept of the long tail does not preclude the emergence of blockbusters. Instead, it suggests that blockbusters will continue to emerge but that they will no longer be exclusively produced by large firms. For example, Tucker and Zhang showed that popularity information (that is, information on the frequency with which a product has been chosen, such as the sales rank on Amazon.com) "may in fact benefit niche products disproportionately."[12]

Large firms have not ignored these market realities. Many have responded by transferring a significant part of their advertising budget to the Web. Several market analysts, such as Nick Brien, CEO of Universal McCann, even predict a massive transfer of budgets. To quote McCann, "big name brand marketers are fed up with traditional media channels and are threatening to shift the lion's share of their budgets online." Brien added that several large firms are "just waiting to increase their online to spend 50% or 60% [of their total budgets]."[13]

Recent statistics, as reported by TNS Media Intelligence, would seem to suggest confirmation of the transfer of advertising expenditures from traditional media to the Web, as shown in the table below.

Percent of Total Expenditures on Types of Advertising

Media	Q1 2008/Q1 2007 (US Market)
Television	2.1%
Magazine	−3.9%
Newspaper	−10.0%
Internet	7.0%
Radio	−8.8%
Outdoor	−0.5%

Source: TNS Media Intelligence, 2008

Taken as a whole, we can see that Google could benefit from the long tail twice: First, with revenue from small advertisers; second, with increasing revenue from the major players striving to keep market share. As Eric Schmidt noted in 2005: "The surprising thing about the Long Tail is just how long the tail is, and how many businesses have been served by traditional advertising sales."[14] And, as he explained in a interview with *The McKinsey Quarterly*, three years later: "While the tail is very interesting, the vast majority of revenue remains in the head."[15]

A significant proportion of revenues is in the head, but only because the long tail has plunged large enterprises into a more competitive world where they have to fight for market share.

PART II
A Formula 1 Engine

Ford invented the $5 day and the moving assembly line, and Toyota became the world's premier manufacturer by revolutionizing inventory management, quality control, and problem solving in manufacturing. Brin, Page, and Schmidt broke barriers that can inhibit innovation and slow growth in large companies by acting on several fronts: people management, product conception, team organization, metrics, and monitoring. They found new ways to motivate and coordinate employees, mobilize innovative resources, and limit the complexity that hinders the rapid release of new products.

3

THREE ICONOCLASTS AT THE TOP

Had the leaders of Google followed the rules and undergone the typical venture capital rite of passage, they would have written a business plan that laid out a detailed financial model showing how they would make money and how long it would take to make a profit for their initial investors.

They did nothing of the sort. Instead, they started by creating user demand and only then did they consider how to generate income.

Is this paradoxical? Undoubtedly. Would this model be difficult to re-create elsewhere? Certainly. In fact, their venture was made possible only because, at the outset, they found confident investors who were willing to wait and because they were brash enough to make their search engine free without first trying to earn money. Their primary goal was to produce high-quality results first—to make Google's search engine so much better than competing engines that it would attract hordes of visitors. And it worked.

Google was undoubtedly lucky: The company was born into a favorable environment, it had patient investors, and it had a large fan club of devoted users on its side. But none of that would have been enough had Google not figured out how to do things differently, starting from the top.

Google built an original system of corporate governance based on a triumvirate that allowed the company to develop and shielded it from shareholder pressures that could have derailed it.

A Triumvirate That Works (Against All Odds)

No management authority would have advised Google to install a triumvirate as top management. When we think of corporate governance, common corporate wisdom tells us to have one leader at the top: a CEO to direct the company and take the fall if things don't go as planned. Triangular relationships have a bad reputation, dating back to the failed triumvirates of ancient Rome.[*]

Strangely enough though, things went well after Page and Brin recruited Eric Schmidt in 2001 from Novell, Inc., where he led strategic planning, management, and technology development as chairman and CEO.

Whereas a typical startup would have divided areas of authority, with Schmidt in charge of the company's management and the co-founders in charge of vision and technology, Page and Brin created a three-headed, power-sharing directorate instead.

---

[*] The Roman Senate engineered two restructurings that created triumvirates to resolve personality conflicts among pretenders to the throne. The first was Julius Caesar, Pompey, and Crassus, and then many years later, Octavian, Mark Antony, and Lepidus. Both attempts were utter failures that led to war.

By all accounts (and against conventional wisdom), this structure has played a critical and positive role on several occasions. The triumvirate approach is so far out of the ordinary that many experts are taken aback—yet it works. Why does the Google triumvirate work when so many others have failed? Its success is probably due in large part to the ability it gives the others to apply the brakes when success inflates the ego of any one of the leaders.

Anyone who has followed leaders in the technology field knows of narcissistic leaders like Bill Gates, Steve Jobs, and Larry Ellison. Certainly these leaders have had tremendous success, but they can also cause tremendous shifts in organizational performance, with their companies experiencing higher highs and lower lows. And they're notoriously difficult to work for.

According to their 2007 study titled "It's All About Me," Chatterjee and Hambrick conclude that narcissism is particularly prevalent among CEOs in the field of new technology.[1] Among Google's three leaders, however, anyone who is tempted to play God is quickly held to account by the checks and balances of the other two leaders.

Google's triumvirate structure also makes reversing errors more quickly possible. A manager alone at the head of a company may be reluctant to correct his or her decisions, even when those decisions are clearly incorrect, due to hubris or a fear of losing his or her position. The triumvirate is less likely to suffer from this problem.

Because a triumvirate shares responsibility, when the triumvirate makes decisions, you can never quite pin down who really made that bad decision, and the likelihood of any one person taking the blame is significantly reduced.

NOTE   *Of course, the triumvirate always runs the risk of two leaders turning against the third one, but when the structure works, it offers significant advantages.*

A triumvirate structure supplies multiple viewpoints, perspectives, and expertise, which can help to reassure investors and customers that someone at the top of the company understands and shares their concerns. For example, Google shareholders may assume that

Schmidt will defend their economic interests, whereas users place confidence in Page and Brin to resist market pressures and to focus the company's direction on producing a quality product.

Finally, a triumvirate can change the balance of power at the top: Three managers can better resist pressure from shareholders and investors than can one person alone.

By adopting this mutual scheme of governance, with oversight by their peers, Google's leaders are freed from outside influences on corporate policies. The pull that middle management, the technocracy, and outside consultants generally exert on large companies, where all decision making is preceded by lengthy discussion and deliberation, is avoided.

As puzzling as this may seem, by agreeing to work under a system of mutual monitoring, Page, Brin, and Schmidt are actually freer. They've loosened constraints that, under the guise of reducing risk and forcing rational decisions, put leaders of most large companies under the control of investors, associates, and advisors. At the same time, they maximize the freedom needed to build a company that doesn't hesitate to break traditional management rules.

As a prerequisite for improving company performance, most treatises on corporate governance emphasize putting strict controls on leaders to limit their room to maneuver. The leaders of Google, however, have been able to find a formula that both preserves broad margins of autonomy for them as a trio and allows them to avoid some of the faults frequently found in leaders who are surrounded by compliant underlings. And, perhaps not least of all, the triumvirate structure guarantees continuity in case one leader should unexpectedly step aside.

How Can Google's Triumvirate Continue to Succeed?

Historically, triumvirates have failed because they were formed to avoid wars of succession, with each player retaining the ambition to become Numero Uno. Most triumvirates set up in modern companies as a result of mergers or acquisitions have suffered the same fate. Google's triumvirate management structure has succeeded so far for these uncommon reasons:

Qualified leadership   All three leaders at Google are qualified to act as top executives. Page and Brin are the company's founders; Schmidt has directed other large companies.

Mutual respect   Eric Schmidt never misses a chance to say how impressed he is by the intelligence of his two younger colleagues.

Shared values   All three leaders of Google are engineers by training. All appreciate the rigor of mathematical reasoning, have confidence in technology, and share the same view of money: They have no problem with making a lot of it, but doing so is not an obsession.

Different perspectives   Each leader has a different perspective. Schmidt is focused on administration; Page pays close attention to the company's social structure; and Brin is in charge of ethical matters. Schmidt is the one who generally speaks to financial analysts, whereas Brin was the spokesperson when it came time to rethink the conditions of entry into the Chinese market.

Only time will tell, of course, but few would argue that Google is off to an inauspicious start.

4

RECRUITING THE BEST

My job can be so exciting. I get to work with some of the brightest minds and most accomplished luminaries in technology, politics, and business. I am consistently humbled and feel lucky for the opportunities I get.[1]

—Christopher Sacca, former Head of Special Initiatives, Google, Inc.

Few companies have expressed so strongly and repeatedly their desire to recruit only the best people. Google's recruitment web pages abound with mantras like "Google seeks to hire only the best." Although reports are that Google has had to relax its hiring policies a bit over the years with its dramatic increase in number of employees, headhunters who have worked with Google make it clear that you have little chance of being hired without a doctorate or at least a master's degree from a top school.

This elitism, the object of ongoing jokes, is not exclusive to Google; the same holds true at Amazon.com and Microsoft. For example, in a 1993 interview, Bill Gates, then CEO of Microsoft, made these remarks, which the owners of Google could repeat verbatim today:

> The key for us, number one, has always been hiring very smart people. There is no way of getting around, that in terms of I.Q., you've got to be very elitist in picking the people who deserve to write software. Ninety-five percent of the people shouldn't write complex software. And using small teams helps a lot. You've got to give great tools to those small teams. So, pick good people, use small teams, give them excellent tools, vast compilation, debugging, lots of machines, profiling technology, so that they are very productive in terms of what they are doing. Make it very clear what they can do to change the spec. Make them feel like they are very much in control of it.[2]

Why the Very Best?

This elitist attitude needs to be considered within the singular context of the technology industry and its fast-growing companies.

At Google, as in all booming firms, a position's scope expands rapidly: An employee may be promoted several times during the years following the start of his or her initial employment. In these circumstances, hiring overqualified people is better. And that means choosing the best.

But that's not the only motive for choosing the best people. Academic qualifications reveal a candidate's psychological profile.

When times are good, tech companies besiege universities trying to hire away their students. Those who remain in school to do graduate work are not only more intelligent and better trained than average—which are already plus points—but also more impassioned and motivated. Immediate money is not their main goal.

These candidates have already shown that they prefer learning to paid employment. The fact that they stayed in school long enough to earn a graduate degree means they already turned down numerous offers to earn fast money as developers—so, in these cases, staying in school long enough to get an advanced degree shows strength of character. Recruiting people with graduate degrees is a way to hire those who are highly motivated and value the quality of their work above their immediate personal interests. In an industry with very high turnover, where fortunes can be made quickly, this factor is important.

Equally important, new hires with graduate degrees are more rigorous in their habits. There's a joke about how doctoral graduates of the École Polytechnique, France's most elite school, put their everyday life into equations. What's certain about recruiting people with PhDs is that they've learned to rely on precise observation, to have confidence in math, to trust rational thought over intuition wherever possible, and to value factual analysis over improvisation. Google looks for these qualities because its co-founders put more confidence in mathematics and rationality than in other qualities.

Finally, the experience of graduate-level research, which is generally done solo, teaches these job candidates to operate autonomously. Each graduate student has had to choose a thesis topic, which familiarized them with what might be called *controlled innovation*. A thesis topic, however original it might be, would have no chance of being accepted if it didn't fall within a certain scope.

So behind this oft-criticized elitism is a realistic motive: The very best employees have a special psychological profile that benefits high tech companies. What would be truly arrogant is the leaders believing that because they are so brilliant themselves they don't need intelligent people around to help develop their company.

A Recruitment Factory

Hiring the best people is usually very expensive. Fortunately for Google, the IT collapse that began in 2000 dumped thousands of trained IT specialists, in all disciplines and at all levels, back into the job market. In 2001, Motorola alone laid off one-quarter of its 150,000 employees. And the search engines weren't doing any better. In January 2001, then-leader AltaVista laid off 250 people, one-fourth of its staff, and canceled its plans to go public. Yahoo!, the other leader in the sector, also suffered large cutbacks. Sun Microsystems, General Electric, and Siemens laid off thousands more, and the list goes on.

Of course, most of those unemployed people didn't go to work for Google, but some of the best ones did. Google was hiring at that time and could recruit from a large applicant pool. Because of the economic situation, Google was able to hire excellent engineers at low starting salaries, with partial compensation in stock options.

As we all know, the economy recovered, and Google's recruitment efforts continued to ramp up aggressively. Rather than settle for the conventional recruiting methods used by most human resources departments (résumé analysis, psychometric tests, and interviews), Google chose a different path—yet again.

The company's reputation, coupled with competitive salary offers, would certainly have enabled it to recruit all the employees it needed. Google's management did something different: They built a veritable recruitment machine, massive to the point of being far disproportionate to the number of employees. In late 2005, Dr. John Sullivan, a human resources expert, reported that 350 people at Google were dedicated to recruitment. With 5,000 employees at the time, this meant that 1 in 14 Google employees was working in recruitment. That's an extremely high ratio, considering that in traditional companies the ratio is 1 recruitment employee per 100 employees. Cisco, another company that is extremely particular about the quality of its new hires, had one recruiter for every 68 employees in 2005.[3]

Of course, these figures are not entirely comparable; not all of Google's in-house recruiters were working full time, and other companies relied more on outside agencies for recruitment. Still, the number of people involved in recruiting was huge, and this most likely continues to be the case.

The human resources department at Google is mostly made up of temporary staffers. The Google recruitment machine is a factory, but a flexible one whose workers are called in as the need arises.

This paradigm is something new in recruiting. In most companies, the size of the recruitment staff remains pretty constant. Procedures adjust to meet workload: Recruitment becomes more complex when fewer open positions exist, and the process is simplified when more openings are available. As a result, the quality of those hired tends to decline as the number of openings (and perhaps the company's desperation) increases. Conversely, the fewer people the company needs to recruit, the more interviews per candidate and the more thorough the process.

Google's recruitment figures show how much importance the company places on a function that most organizations neglect or deal with in a haphazard way. And for good reason: In a fast-growing company that hires a lot of people, the quality of the workforce is at stake and can very quickly deteriorate.

The mechanism is simple. Allow average employees to recruit coworkers, and they will likely choose those who won't outshine them. This leads to a bureaucratic organization clogged with people who lack the authority to make the slightest decisions without seeking the approval of those above them. This phenomenon is an all-too-common one that has even given rise to a proverb in Silicon Valley, pointed out repeatedly by Ram Shriram,* one of Google's first investors and now a member of the board of directors: "Hire only A people, and they'll hire other A people. If you hire a B person, they'll hire C or D people." Forgetting this rule leads to sloppiness in very fast-growing companies. And Google has been particularly fast growing: At the end of 2003, Google had 1,628 employees, a number that grew to 10,674 by the end of 2006. That increase of over 9,000 employees represents a more than five-fold increase in only three years. And, as of June 2008, Google had 19,604 full-time

---

* Before starting his own venture capital firm, Shriram was one of the original team at Netscape, held an executive position at Amazon.com, and founded several startup companies.

employees—nearly double the number of employees that it had at the end of 2006. As Peter Norvig, Director of Google Research, explains:

> But how do you maintain the skill level while roughly doubling in size each year? We rely on the Lake Wobegon Strategy, which says *only hire candidates who are above the mean of your current employees*. An alternative strategy (popular in the dot-com boom period) is to justify a hire by saying "this candidate is clearly better than at least one of our current employees."[4]

Evaluating Technical Expertise

On the surface, Google's recruitment process looks similar to those of other companies. Like Microsoft and most large technology firms, Google gives candidates a more or less traditional series of tests.

Those applying for a technical position take the Google Labs Aptitude Test (GLAT), which is distinguished not only by its difficulty (with some fairly complex statistical and mathematical questions) but also by its originality and humor. For example, here's a sample question taken from an actual GLAT:

> On your first day at Google, you discover that your cubicle mate wrote the textbook you used as a primary resource in your first year of graduate school. Do you:
>
> A) Fawn obsequiously and ask if you can have an autograph.
>
> B) Sit perfectly still and use only soft keystrokes to avoid disturbing her concentration.
>
> C) Leave her daily offerings of granola and English toffee from the food bins.
>
> D) Quote your favorite formula from the textbook and explain how it's now your mantra.
>
> E) Show her how example 17b could have been solved with 34 fewer lines of code.[5]

Once the tests are passed, interviews follow. Nothing about the process is casual.

Only in the details does the originality of this process become apparent, however. The first difference is in its organization. At other companies, recruiters generally use only a small number of tools: specialized employment agencies, print ads, job fairs, contacts with schools and professors, and headhunters whose main expertise is in building networks of contacts.

Google uses those tools, too, but it also relies on its academic culture and its experience in the field of research (both in terms of database searching and research within a university environment). Its Summer of Code, a program that offers student developers stipends to write code for various open source projects, allows human resources to identify candidates capable of resolving complex problems. Google also sponsors contests that attract the most brilliant minds in the field. And Google uses its own search tools to identify people who are interested in its job openings.

Another hallmark of Google's recruitment strategy is *recruiter specialization*. The recruitment process is managed and organized along particular roles. Some recruiters specialize only in first jobs, others in technical people or managers, and still others speak only to candidates for overseas employment. Even at the largest companies, finding such specialization in the field of human resources would be rare.

The result is that each recruiter sees only a very narrow sector of candidates, so he or she can evaluate them closely to select those who will be asked to take the psychometric tests and then, if they pass the tests, be called in for interviews.

The most original part of recruitment at Google is the actual selection process. During this process, Google brings in future coworkers for multiple, lengthy interviews—as many as eight interviews per potential new hire. (This information comes from candidates who weren't hired, because those who get jobs are bound by a lengthy confidentiality agreement.)

By all accounts, the process is similar to university seminars where a candidate is examined by peer experts who ask him or her technical questions. They don't ask about his or her personality or ability to get along in a group; they want to know about the candidate's capabilities. The questions are technical, challenging, and very close to the topic at hand. The interview is a strict evaluation of the candidate's technical competence and his or her ability to comprehend, address, and resolve the company's technological challenges.

And when the peers asking the questions don't have the know-how to evaluate the answers (as must happen often), they can at least pose questions that will help form a clearer opinion. Greg Linden, one of the creators of Amazon.com, explains it this way:

> . . . exploring someone's knowledge doesn't necessarily require knowledge of it yourself. You can just keep asking questions, diving deeper and deeper. If they really understand the problem, they should be able to explain it to others, to teach people about the problem. Eventually, you should get to a point where they say "I don't know" to a question. That's a great sign. Knowing what you know isn't as important as knowing what you don't know. It is a sign of real understanding when someone can openly discuss where their knowledge ends.[6]

During these discussions, the questions tackled are real ones that arise within the company. One famous example is a question from Amin Saberi's interview; Saberi was a student in the final year of the IT doctorate program at the Georgia Institute of Technology.

In one interview, Monika Henzinger, then Director of Research, asked if he had any ideas about how to improve the ad rankings on Google's pages. The question was minor, but back at the university, the young researcher mentioned it to his thesis advisor, who recommended exploring it. After some study, they decided that it would work better to include the daily budget of the advertiser within the ranking algorithm. Saberi and his colleagues wrote the algorithm and filed a patent.[7]

This sort of question is a long way from traditional evaluation methods used in small firms, which often base their methods on intuition and empathy.* But Google's process is just as far from the

---

* Interviews of this sort can become pretty intense. A former Apple employee related how Steve Jobs upset a candidate whom he found a bit uptight by asking if he was still a virgin. Needless to say, the candidate concluded he wasn't the right guy for the job. (Andy Hertzfeld, "Gobble, Gobble, Gobble," *http://www.folklore.org/*)

formal evaluations used by large companies, which attempt to evaluate a prospective employee's personality as well as his or her ability to fit into the professional environment. At Google, a candidate must convince his or her future peers that he or she can solve the problems encountered in the everyday work environment. That is all that counts.

If, on the surface, Google's recruitment procedures resemble those of other major companies, it becomes obvious, when looking at the details, that their methods are actually the opposite of traditional ones:

- Recruitment is considered a major function, which is rarely the case.

- Human resource staffing is flexible so it can quickly be adapted to meet current need.

- Degrees and academic qualifications are used to evaluate personal qualities such as chosen career path, rigor in reasoning, and autonomy. Normally, degrees are used only to evaluate technical expertise.

- Interviews are used to examine technical qualifications: Candidates are asked questions that apply to the work environment.

These ideas contribute to Google's success. Can they be applied anywhere? I'm not so sure. Google's hiring process has one main shortcoming: It is very, very long. So long that Google's specialists decided to limit the number of interviews candidates went through. They also asked staff members who interview candidates to submit their assessment within a week.[8] And if Google's process is too long for Google, it's definitely too long for companies that don't have its magnetic pull. In most cases, candidates won't wait several months before receiving an answer.

5

THE 20 PERCENT RULE

Recruiting the best people is good; keeping them is a lot better. This is why Google works so hard to offer its employees more than just financial motivation.

Psychologists who study employee behavior define two types of motivation: external, or extrinsic, and internal, or intrinsic. *Intrinsic* motivation comes from within the employee, from the employee's interest in a task, and the satisfaction that comes from doing a job well. *Extrinsic* motivation comes from outside the employee, essentially from rewards such as bonuses, raises, or changes in responsibilities.

Like other companies, Google uses external motivators. Many Google employees are making plenty of money, as you can easily see by counting the luxury cars in the parking lot. But Google also relies heavily on intrinsic motivation, because the company recognizes that its employees are motivated by more than money.

By doing so, Google follows well-known principles like those expressed by Bill Gates early in his career: "No great programmer is sitting there saying, 'I'm going to make a bunch of money,' or 'I'm going to sell a hundred thousand copies.' Because that kind of thought gives you no guidance about the problems."[1]

Google no doubt found it easy to see how well developers respond to intrinsic motivation. As an example, Google could look to the desire to produce quality software as evidenced by the open source community, which depends on the cooperation and contributions of thousands of talented programmers who donate their time to develop and improve software. Their motivation comes largely from a desire to produce quality software to be given away for free.

Still, Google had to adapt this type of intrinsic incentive to a corporate environment. Google's approach was to reinvent an approach that the 3M company adopted in its research centers. 3M's 15 percent rule encourages its researchers to devote 15 percent of their time to projects of their own choosing, in other words to "experimental doodling," as 3M's former Chairman of the Board William McKnight called it. The 15 percent rule has been the source of several highly profitable products, including Scotchgard Fabric & Upholstery Protector, Scotch Masking Tape, and the highly profitable Post-it Notes. Hewlett-Packard has a similar policy.

Google's stated policy splits the work hours of its engineers and developers into two parts: Eighty percent of their time is dedicated to assigned projects, the official source of their paycheck, with the remaining 20 percent dedicated to personal research of their own choosing.

The 20 percent policy is a boon for employees who have never had a moment to spare at previous jobs, and it's also gratifying to managers who can stop nagging employees about "soldiering on."

Although originally conceived by 3M to reduce turnover among engineers who wanted to develop concepts they dreamed up at work, this policy is one of the mainstays of the Google innovation machine. When an employee envisions a new product, managers don't say, "It's not a priority, so don't waste your time on it."

That is the exact answer Steve Wozniak, co-founder of Apple Computer, got from Hewlett-Packard management when he proposed developing a personal computer. Today, Google would presumably tell him, "You can devote 20 percent of your time to it."

NOTE   *Of course, although the engineers are free to choose which area of research they want to pursue, Google assumes their research will mainly be aligned with the company's goals.*

Functionally, the 20 percent strategy offers several advantages in today's business environment. The strategy makes Google attractive to young college graduates (and potential hires) who want to preserve some degree of the autonomy they enjoyed in academia as they enter the corporate world. What better way for a company to make a good first impression than by allowing recent graduates to allocate 20 percent of their time to the development of their own projects?

The 20 percent rule also attracts those who contribute to the open source community; they see it as an opportunity to continue their projects (and possibly "sell" them to Google). For example, consider these thoughts from Mike Pinkerton, the principal developer of the Macintosh web browser Camino. When Pinkerton began working at Google, in September 2005, he wrote in his blog:

> What oh what does it mean for Camino now that Pink is going to work on Firefox? The answer: only good things. Remember that Google employees get 20% of their time to work on their own pet projects. While some of that time will hopefully be spent nurturing the growing Mac community within Google, a lot of that time will be directly spent on Camino. That's right, I'm (indirectly) getting paid to keep working on it. That's going to be a big help with the push for 1.0 coming up this Fall.[2]

Google's 20 percent policy (and 3M's 15 percent policy before it) also enhances productivity. Engineers are motivated to work faster in order to free up their personal creative time, while Google's overall culture of quality insures that 80 percent of work won't be slipshod. And connections between Google's engineers and academic acquaintances are encouraged because part of their time at Google can be spent on work that may lead to publication in academic journals.

The 20 percent policy also leads to the emergence of new Google products, especially ones that Google can integrate into its current offerings. Google Suggest, AdSense for Content, and Orkut are direct results of this 20 percent rule. What Google gives with one hand, it recovers with the other.

The 20 percent rule makes perfect business sense and is consistent with the logic of the potlatch, or reciprocity of gift giving, as discussed in Chapter 2. This rule is also consistent with Nobel Prize–winning economist George Akerlof's observations in a paper that he published in 1984 titled "Gift Exchange and Efficiency Wage Theory."[3]

Akerlof was surprised to see certain companies paying employees higher-than-market salaries. Based upon his research and analysis, he concluded that the companies weren't paying higher wages because they were irrational or ignorant, but rather they were attempting to reduce turnover (which is expensive) and increase productivity and efficiency. They also knew that their employees would make extra efforts to thank them for their generosity. Similarly, Google's assumption is that the 20 percent free time it gives its employees will be returned to the company in information, innovation, and increased loyalty.

Of course, this unusual HR policy requires new administrative practices. In service businesses like consulting or engineering, employees fill out timesheets with charges that detail how many hours they spent on a given project. At Google, employees are asked to report in about five sentences how they used their time the previous week and to share their projects with coworkers for peer review. If the employee's peers find the project promising, it is adopted as an official, company-financed project.

With personal projects subject to peer review, the quality bar is again set high. Essentially, the resulting peer pressure and the value that employees place on their professional reputation ensures that employees will take their personal projects quite seriously and that priority will be given to ideas that are likely to interest the company and be highly regarded.

The 20 percent rule also tends to weed out underperforming employees and reinforce dedication to assigned work. Employees are under a lot of internal pressure to demonstrate progress with their personal projects, and employees that show little progress are seen as perhaps not being up to the Google standard. In sum, Google's 20 percent rule results in three indirect forms of leverage over its engineers:

- I owe something to the company because I'm given the freedom to invent and develop my own ideas.

- If I can't free up 20 percent of my time, my performance is below par.

- My reputation depends on developing ideas that will earn my colleagues' respect.

Judging by the comments of some former employees, the 20 percent rule is extremely effective.

So is Google a worker's paradise? Free meals, massages, swimming pools, sports facilities, coworkers traveling between offices on scooters or Segways. Many have described the generous benefits available to employees at the Googleplex.

When journalists question the value of these perks, company executives say something like, "Well, come around at 2 AM and see how many people are at the office." No journalist has been curious enough to verify that statement, so saying exactly how many people are at their desk in the middle of the night is difficult, but the statement's implication doesn't sound too farfetched. Hackers are known for keeping irregular schedules and working for long stretches without watching the clock. They produce best during prolonged periods of uninterrupted work, as Joseph Weizenbaum writes in his *Computer Power and Human Reason*: "The compulsive programmer spends all the time he can working on one of his big projects."[4] He then goes so far as to compare hackers to the compulsive gamblers described by Dostoyevsky:

> for whom nothing exists but roulette . . . who scarcely notice what goes on around them, being interested in nothing else, who do nothing but play from morning 'til night, and would probably continue all night nonstop if they could.[5]

The environment Google provides gives employees with unusual work habits the means to regain their equilibrium after working long hours. Although the environment is less about paradise than about health and fitness, Google is paradise nonetheless for many employees.

6

COWORKERS ARE THE BEST JUDGES

Articles written about Google mention its peer review policy less frequently than its 20 percent rule, but the peer review policy is at least as important in filtering out the best projects for development and feeding Google's innovation pipeline.

As mentioned in Chapter 5, a team with a prospective project that is an outgrowth of the 20 percent rule presents the project for coworkers from other departments to review. In a traditional company, such a review would be the province of top executives, the marketing department, or an executive committee. But at Google, peer review takes place within a committee composed of coworkers. Like an academic peer review group, this committee meets frequently to decide whether to adopt new projects and to monitor those already underway. The meetings are reportedly brief and intense:

> Most Fridays at Google, the search-engine company in Mountain View, California, Marissa Mayer and about 50 engineers and other employees sit down to do a search of their own. Mayer, an intense, fast-talking product manager, scribbles rapidly as the engineers race to explain and defend the new ideas that they've posted to an internal Web site. By the end of the hour-long meeting, six, seven, or sometimes even eight new ideas are fleshed out enough to take to the next level of development. Some of those ideas might become new features on Google, new code or search algorithms, or a new way to juice up the Google home page. "We really jam in there," Mayer says.[1]

This method is largely inspired by the peer review process used for scientific journals. The editorial boards of scientific journals, typically composed of a panel of recognized experts in the field, review and critique the work that scientists submit to them for publication. When the editorial board meets, these opinions (which may often be quite harsh) are discussed and shared, and the board makes a collective decision to publish or not. Similarly, Google employees submit their work to their peers, high-level engineers whose opinions are respected throughout the company because of their achievements and expertise. Their opinion counts, and getting their approval is important to everyone.

The Power of Reputation

Applied to the corporate world, this method focuses communication directly and exclusively on the topic at hand, such as code or programming. Better yet, the outcome depends not on seniority, but on brainpower, qualifications, and fluency in the language of technology. The judges are people who can read a page of code and spot weaknesses.

These peer reviews contribute to the creation of a parallel hierarchy based on a person's reputation for technical expertise. Eric Schmidt stressed the importance of this in an interview with *Fast Company* magazine in 1999, when he was still head of Novell. In this article, "How to Manage Geeks," Schmidt describes the notion of a "technical career ladder" that would put people on track to become distinguished engineers:

> If you don't want to lose your geeks, you have to find a way to give them promotions without turning them into managers. Most of them are not going to make very good executives—and, in fact, most of them would probably turn out to be terrible managers. But you need to give them a forward career path, you need to give them recognition, and you need to give them more money.

> Twenty years ago, we developed the notion of a dual career ladder, with an executive career track on one side and a technical career track on the other. Creating a technical ladder is a big first step. But it's also important to have other kinds of incentives, such as awards, pools of stock, and non-financial types of compensation. At Novell, we just added a new title: distinguished engineer. To become a distinguished engineer, you have to get elected by your peers. That requirement is a much tougher standard than being chosen by a group of executives. It's also a standard that encourages tech people to be good members of the tech community. It acts to reinforce good behavior on everyone's part.[2]

In this way, Google appeals to the hacker mindset—these are the technology fanatics the company wants to recruit. The assumption is that geeks are not rewarded by giving them managerial titles. Yes, monetary rewards are important, but nonfinancial types of compensation are at least as important. Peer review and respect count for an awful lot.

This peer review approach harks back to the principle of competition for honor, which was popular in the literature of the 18th-century Enlightenment; *competition for honor* was a central theme in the analyses of merit by Helvétius, Diderot, and the Encyclopédistes. They described merit as being derived from relationships of mutual esteem rather than tokens of honor handed down from above: "True glory consists in the regard of people who are themselves worthy of regard, and only this regard equates to merit," wrote the author of the article "Esteem" in Diderot's *Encyclopédie*.* Or as Montesquieu explained in Book III of his *Spirit of Laws*, "Honour sets all the parts of the body politic in motion, and by its very action connects them; thus each individual advances the public good, while he only thinks of promoting his own interest."[3]

This "competition for honor" provides an elegant solution to a problem common to all companies that employ skilled specialists: How do you increase organizational bureaucracy while simultaneously providing opportunities for high-level engineers without shuttling them into management positions that will only prevent them from doing what they do best?

A Tool for Quality Control

Peer review is also a formidable force for ensuring quality. It supports the most important principles of programming—standardized development and quality control—because accepted projects must meet accepted standards.

Repeated, detailed discussions among colleagues regarding company programs encourage the natural development of a common vernacular. Any urge toward nonstandard development will be nipped in the bud, as nobody wants to risk having his or her project fail the peer review test. Everyone knows that their peers are sure to reject a project that doesn't fit the vernacular.

This process solves one of the biggest problems software companies face when they innovate: building a Tower of Babel, with lines of products and modules that can't communicate, which can be expensive both in terms of actual cost and inflexibility. Future development will be not only more costly but also limited by the fact that knowledge remains locked in the memories of the developers who created the code; in effect, development becomes proprietary.

---

* A group of 18th-century intellectuals led by Diderot collaborated to compile the first encyclopedia of science. The project took 26 years to complete (1751–1777), with more than 140 authors writing 70,000 articles. Their *Encyclopédie* contained 26 volumes of text and 11 volumes of illustrative engravings.

As "owners" of the program, these programmers become indispensable. No one else can upgrade or maintain the software. This creates problems whenever management wants to reassign team members, terminate employees, or simply negotiate salary increases.

Peer reviews also encourage thorough source code documentation. Traditionally, programmers have resisted documenting their code because the process is time consuming and it interrupts their workflow. Instead, they put documenting aside until later, which often means never.

Programmers subject to peer review, however, must show their colleagues the algorithm or program modules they are writing. They are required to document their code as they write it, with the documentation itself becoming a means of quality control. Quality is no longer the domain of inspectors, as is standard practice within a traditional company. Instead the quality control is enacted by the labor force itself, along the lines of the Toyota model.

Using peer reviews has other subtle benefits, too. For one, it modifies management practices and the organizational hierarchy, simplifying large projects by dividing them into smaller pieces. Peers may be unwilling to examine a very long program because doing so might require too great an investment of their time.

As in scientific publishing, where peer review is used to vet articles before they are assembled into books, Google's peer reviewers have less work to do when projects are subdivided. (This mode of evaluation also enables Google to track development more closely and to cancel a project sooner if it isn't viable.)

Obviously, this model has serious advantages in terms of improved quality, exchanges among engineers, and product management. But the model is not perfect. Two key areas are vulnerable. First, a considerable amount of time and energy must be expended. Second, the model has a political aspect. Unlike the peer review system used in the academic world, Google's is not anonymous. The reviewers, referees, and experts in charge of evaluating projects all know one another and often work together.

The political aspect leads to intrigue. When participants are not invited to peer review meetings, the rumor mill buzzes with talk of future pink slips.

But then again, every company has its unique corporate culture, and each has its particular quirks and oddities. Like any company, Google is not immune to these potential problems and corporate intrigues. Although the company trades in data and information, Google is full of people, and where there are people, there is politics.

7

AN INNOVATION MACHINE

If asked to describe Google in a few words, you might call it "an innovation machine." Hardly a month goes by, often not even a week, without an announcement from Google regarding some sort of new release.

Anyone in the tech industry knows that innovation is essential, and the fact that Google innovates is certainly nothing new. But what Google understands better than other companies is that innovation for the sake of innovation isn't enough to protect a company from increasing competition.

As you'll recall from Chapter 1, software receives weak intellectual property protection, and California's liberal legal climate disallows noncompete clauses in employment contracts. New ideas don't remain new for long before they face direct competition.

In fact, the time between the release of a new product and the appearance of direct competition has shrunken dramatically over the years. In 2001, economists Rajshree Agarwal and Michael Gort calculated the interval between the appearance of a new product and the arrival in the market of a directly competing product over a 100-year period from 1886 to 1986. Their result is telling: As shown in the figure below, these intervals have shortened continually—to the point of nearly disappearing—from about 25 years at the beginning of the 20th century to less than five years between 1947 and 1986.[1]

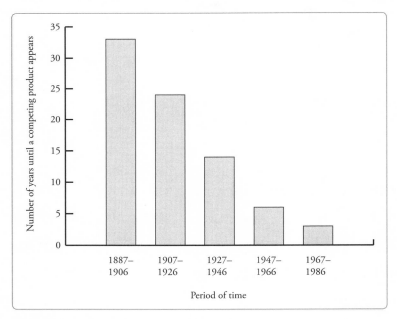

Time until appearance of competing products

Whereas the time between the release of new products and the appearance of direct competition has decreased dramatically, the cost of innovation, including research and development (R&D),

has only increased. In fact, in the 30 years between 1958 and 1988, these costs increased sevenfold in the United States.

The moral of this story is that today no company can rely on a single technological breakthrough to ensure its future.

In the past, companies like Kodak, Xerox, and Polaroid could preserve their market dominance for decades with patents. Now, companies that want to beat the competition and build a dominant position must find other methods.

But how? One response to the challenge is to increase the pace of new product releases to stay ahead of the competition. Judging by its constant flow of new products and features, Google seems to have decided to go this route. Its leaders must have deduced early on that stopping with the first version of their search engine would be suicidal, even if the engine was considered infinitely better than its competitors. Their algorithm was likely to encounter competition unless it evolved quickly, and without a doubt, that competition is right around the corner. According to Marissa Mayer, Vice President of Search Products and User Experience at Google, "We were constantly searching for new ideas."[2]

Ideas are quickly transformed into products because Google is not restrained by traditional R&D procedures. The company keeps listening, always and everywhere, because it knows that breakthrough ideas can come from anyone—engineers, academics, even competitors. And when it comes to good ideas, Google knows that no one is superior, and no one person has an edge, not even the company's leaders.

Don't Formalize Research

Individual geniuses toiling in solitude are not the source of most inventions—large corporations are. And as anyone who has worked at a large corporation knows, that progress actually comes about through the bureaucratic process.

Most corporations give birth to new projects only after following a regulated, formal, and complex set of routines. Now, I'm oversimplifying a bit, but basically the process works like this: Researchers devote countless hours to drafting documents for committees to examine at great length before making even the smallest decisions.

These committees project the rate of return on investment (often based on pure conjecture), and if the proposed project passes this first stage, the researchers work with the marketing department to determine the product's specifications. Proposals that do not fit neatly within the company's strategic mandates are abandoned, with the rest bounced back to researchers with requests for more details and further explanation. That's the routine.

Of course, this method has its advantages. Its advocates defend it with good cause, saying it reduces the risk of developing new products and prevents the development of products the company couldn't market anyway.

Anyone familiar with the history of technology has heard about the mishaps at the Xerox PARC research facility in Palo Alto. This famous think tank developed several important new technologies, including Ethernet and the graphical user interface that inspired the Apple Macintosh. But how could a photocopier company have manufactured and marketed leading-edge computer products? The end result was that the inventions of Xerox's engineers either remained in their filing cabinet or were plundered by competitors better equipped to market them.

If the slow product release track has its advantages, it also has major defects: It consumes vast amounts of time and money, and it faces major stumbling blocks from the bureaucracy itself. Management is wary of taking risks. Operations people hate to eliminate products they already manufacture and distribute because they don't want to discard their investment in manufacturing, advertising, and sales training. The legal department worries about liability. Although none of these precautions is illogical, cumulatively they increase costs, raise break-even points, and limit innovation.

How does Google do it differently? Its founders have chosen to simplify the product development process. For one thing, many decisions are made in the peer reviews described in Chapter 6, thus dramatically reducing paperwork.

Two criteria are emphasized over any others (including compliance with the business plan): technical feasibility and user interest. Projects need not be part of a three- or five-year program in order to be pursued. If they're feasible and meet users' needs, they have a good shot of succeeding. This approach has a reverse effect: Product introductions don't follow any apparent logic, which can give the impression that the company is going off in every direction, chasing several rabbits at once. But it prevents ideas from being neglected—ideas whose only defect is that they don't fit within a predetermined framework. Those that are retained can go into development at once. The *a priori* operational control exerted by management is absent for projects developed during the 20 percent personal-time allotment. The benefits are immediate in terms of both time expended and time to market. Engineers aren't forced to spend additional development time, and they save the time needed to generate paperwork arguments that others would spend yet more time demolishing.

Innovation Is Everybody's Business

Routines are a natural outgrowth of specialized research. When product development is entrusted to specialists, management wants to be able to control them. The only way to do this is to establish procedures. By making innovation everybody's business, Google reduced this tendency in the simplest way possible, according to Marissa Mayer. In practice, this means Google's culture values original ideas from any employee, and any engineer can quickly develop a major product advance during his or her 20 percent free time. Examples of these successes include Google News, which was the idea of Krishna Bharat, an Indian engineer who was fascinated that his grandfather tuned in to the BBC every day to compare British commentary with what he read in the Indian press. The same goes for Orkut, Google's social networking community, as well as the Google Toolbar that keeps track of recent searches on Google.

The famous Japanese quality circles of the 1970s confirmed the ability of individual employees to contribute to improvements in production methods. But even before quality circles received so much attention, many industrial companies solicited suggestions for improvements from employees. Some gave awards for the soundest, most original, or most profitable proposals.

To trace the genealogy of this concept, you have to go back to Adam Smith and his account in *The Wealth of Nations* of the invention of one of the most significant improvements to the steam engine:

> In the first fire [steam] engines, a boy was constantly employed to open and shut the valves as the piston ascended or descended. One of those boys observed that, by tying a string from the handle of the valve to another part of the machine, the valve would open and shut without assistance, and leave him to divert himself with his play-fellows. One of the greatest improvements was thus the discovery of a boy who wanted to save his own labour. . . .[3]

This concept may be simple and obvious, but its implementation is limited. The toolboxes used in quality circles are mostly empty; quality circles only refine the details. Google's leaders figured out what many others missed, so they created an environment favorable to innovation, and they installed tools to help new ideas emerge. In startup companies, the original core staff members are typically the ones most closely involved in product development. The founders generally have a yearning for innovation and new ideas, or they would be working someplace else. They also share a direct bond with the company's leaders, which makes communicating new ideas and seeking their endorsement easy. But as companies grow and become more bureaucratic, things change. They become more risk averse, relationships are politicized, and ideas often disappear in the management layers as a result. Google has managed to avoid the bureaucratic trap only because of the subtle—and no doubt fragile—concept for innovation developed by its leaders. The formula looks like this:

Recruit only the brightest, most qualified engineers from top universities. Management can more easily accept ideas from highly educated developers than from employees with no academic qualifications.

Encourage the collaboration of Internet enthusiasts. Their opinions and ideas can only be useful.

Build networks of Silicon Valley contacts. Stay connected. Listen to find out what competing companies and startups are working on.

Encourage everyone to seek a place in the web inventor hall of fame. As respected tech essayist Paul Graham wrote, "What matters in Silicon Valley is how much effect you have on the world. The reason people there care about Larry and Sergey is not their wealth but the fact that they control Google, which affects practically everyone."[4]

Facilitate the rapid circulation of ideas throughout the company. Google supports communication among teams working on different projects with networking tools. These include the intranet, blogs, and even the office design itself. A grand Brazilian hardwood staircase in the main lobby is fitted with electrical outlets so employees can sit on the steps and share their work with others. Did the architect come up with this idea? No. Larry Page was personally involved in the office design and construction. He knew how much the working environment could support the exchange of ideas and experience that are behind so many innovations.

Look for Ideas Where They Are

You've seen how Google motivates its engineers to seek new ideas and share them. But its leaders haven't stopped there. They've also built a company able to look for ideas wherever they may be—whether at a university, among the users of the programs it freely provides to developers, or in other companies.

Consider Amin Saberi, who was in his last year at the Georgia Institute of Technology when he was involved in developing the keyword auction algorithm discussed in Chapter 4. The problem posed during an interview reminded him, a fellow student, and his thesis advisor (a Berkeley alumnus) of a more general pairing problem that had been solved 15 years earlier. They applied their knowledge to the algorithm, and a few weeks later presented the result at a Stanford conference attended by Google employees, who subsequently invited them to present their algorithm at the Googleplex.

Collaborating with universities comes naturally for a company with many young recent graduates. Many of Google's employees maintain close links to their alma maters and connections with friends at other creative companies. These connections help to keep Google in touch with new developments elsewhere.

For example, Google's desktop search resulted from a conversation between friends in which one mentioned an Australian engineer who had created a search engine to find local files on his Linux computer. This tip drove the development of Google Desktop and gave Google a two-month lead on Microsoft's similar tool. Remember, when the interval between a new product release and the launch of a competing product is shrinking, time is of the essence.

More ideas come from the programmers that Google regularly solicits through contests like the code competition held every summer since 2002.* The first prize includes $10,000 cash, an all-expense-paid VIP visit to the Googleplex in Mountain View, and a potential trial run of the code on Google's multibillion-document repository. In 2006, Google received more than 3,000 applications; of those, 630 were from students at 456 universities. Students from 90 different countries were represented in the competition.

The first winner of the programming contest, Daniel Egnor, entered a search application that would display only local results. For example, if you were looking for a mechanic in San Francisco, the search engine would display only pages of San Francisco–based mechanics. This was the origin of Google Local, a service that now competes with the local Yellow Pages and other local search services in the United States.

Google also knows that its users have great ideas, too. One example is the Professor-Verifier, a program developed by an academic using one of the application programming interfaces (APIs) that Google gives away to its customers. The application makes it easy to check academic credentials: Enter a name in the search box, and the program automatically queries all university sites. If the name appears on one of the sites, the tool confirms that the person is who he or she says. If the name doesn't appear, maybe the person isn't who he or she says. From here, you can easily see how Google could build an extension to this application that would, for example, check the academic qualifications of employment candidates.

* Contest information is available at *http://www.google.com/programming-contest/winner.html*.

Acquire

Finally, Google excels at buying ideas (see the table below). Unlike many other industry players (especially Apple, which is known for developing its products exclusively in-house), Google is known for buying companies with interesting products. Since 2001, the search giant has acquired over 50 companies. Most of them are startups created by small teams, often as few as two or three people, with an idea and the ability to develop it. Typically, acquisition targets have been companies that have developed a new web application that has attracted a few thousand or tens of thousands of visitors.

Google Acquisitions from 2001 through 2008

Year	Number of Acquisitions	Fields
2001	2	Data mining, search engine
2003	6	Search engine, online advertising, blogging
2004	6	Traffic and map analysis, image organizer, HTML editor, search engine
2005	10	Broadband Internet access, graphic software, search engines, mobile and graphic software, office automation software
2006	11	Advertising, blogging software, video sharing (YouTube), computer vision, office automation software
2007	16	Office automation software, advertising, statistical software, advertising, photography, social networking
2008	3	Online advertising, online video, weblog software

Sources: The Net Journal (August 24, 2005), CNET, and Wikipedia

This type of growth is external, but not the same kind of external growth produced by acquiring other Internet players. In the late 1990s, when Yahoo! acquired several competing search engines (including AltaVista and Overture), its objective was to consolidate the field. This same traditional policy of consolidation led Oracle to acquire PeopleSoft, the human resources software company. Google, however, acquires for innovation, not consolidation. Rather than reinvent what already exists, Google shops and buys appropriate tools when it can. This strategy sidesteps the "not invented here" syndrome that has been so costly for many companies stuck in the paradigm of copying what others have invented.

Google acquires more than market share, expertise, or even technology when it acquires a company. After all, Google already has the means and the engineers to emulate or reinvent these products; instead, it "buys" the users and sometimes the founders.

Consider Google's acquisition of PyraLabs in 2003. The company was a pioneer in the field of blogs. Google could easily have developed its own blogging software (the resources and technology would certainly have been easy for them to replicate), but Google lacked the user base. Purchasing PyraLabs gave Google not only a blogging tool but also dedicated users.

YouTube is another example. Google had already developed its own video upload service when it spent $1.65 billion to acquire the fledgling company in October 2006. But YouTube had been first to market and already had a committed, massive, and growing user base.

In both cases, Google needed an important asset that it couldn't necessarily produce on its own: subscribers and information on the behavior of those subscribers. The search engine looks for what Internet users want without going through the process of market research. Of course, you may wonder why these mostly young companies agree to be bought. Cash is one reason, but not the only one. By acquiring these companies, Google gives their leaders an opportunity that no venture capital firm could offer: They gain access to Google's platform, its statistical capability, and its expertise—plus its aura of chutzpah.

Release Early and Often (or, How to Involve Users in the Development Process)

The last component of the Google innovation machine is its early release of new products. Instead of waiting until its products are refined, Google releases them as beta versions. To avoid making waves among more cautious users, Google says little or nothing about upgrades to its tools; they typically just appear ready to be discovered. Bloggers are the main communication source about new tools.

This silence enables the company to divide its users into two main segments: early adopters and mainstream users. Early adopters include the adventurous pioneers, who are usually the best qualified, most interested, and most interesting to the company. Early adopters tend to be tolerant of product flaws because they understand that a beta product is likely to have bugs. They try the upgrade, evaluate it, and help improve it. Mainstream users, on the other hand, tend to be more cautious users who need some time to become familiar with upgrades.

This strategy makes it possible to multiply new releases without generating many complaints. Google can identify defects and make quiet improvements. For instance, only the initial users of Google Books learned in February 2006 that the software for displaying book pages contained a bug. By the time most people discovered the service, the bug had been fixed.

Google's release strategy brings the concept of *bootstrapping* to the business world. Bootstrapping is a concept developed by researchers at the Augmentation Research Center,[*] a Stanford University laboratory. The expression derives from stories told about the (real) Baron von Münchhausen, who (the stories go) pulled himself out of a swamp by tugging on his bootstraps.

Google bootstraps its early products by sharing them with researchers, requesting feedback, and using that feedback to enhance features. By doing so, it augments its narrow development team by inviting more adventurous users, either self-selected or recruited by friends and relatives within the community, to join its Trusted Tester Program, a little-known program that acts as a sort of private club for friends of Google employees. This program allows invited individuals to test confidential Google products during early development stages.

This early release and testing strategy not only shortens development time, but also delegates to privileged user "volunteers" the responsibility of product testing—evaluating performance, identifying flaws, and suggesting improvements.

---

[*] This laboratory was founded by Douglas Engelbart, one of the fathers of the Internet. He invented the mouse, a standard feature of all personal computers today. He was also the first to use a cathode ray tube to display text and graphs, which makes him the inventor of the monitor.

Obviously, the approach incorporates one of the founding principles of the open source movement. In fact, Google uses the "release early, release often" policy pioneered by that community, specifically by Linus Torvalds, the creator of Linux.

Involving users in the product development process is not without its risks. The trade press and bloggers are sometimes scornful, or at least skeptical, of these beta products. For example, influential blogger Dave Pell's comment in January 2006 about the Google video service, "Hey, is it my imagination, or is [this] the first really bad product Google has launched?" caused quite a buzz. His criticism was picked up by CNET and reverberated across the Internet.

But, in the end, negative critiques like this one don't really matter. These reactions ultimately serve to provide Google with useful information on how to improve their product offerings. Users judge the performance of its products over the long term and overlook occasional mistakes; they also tend to become more tolerant as the fixes appear.

The fact that users don't pay for most Google services undoubtedly influences their behavior. They are encouraged to try applications they otherwise wouldn't buy and to participate and reciprocate with comments or advice, whether negative or constructive. Most users don't even notice new releases until weeks after they've been launched (and improved, if need be). This limits the impact of a potential error. Beyond these advantages, the early release policy allows Google to circumvent the bureaucracy of traditional industrial research methodology and profit from its investments in R&D.

By bringing products to market rapidly, whether they're ready or not, Google derives maximum benefit from its efforts and short-circuits potential competition. After all, profitability doesn't come from innovation alone. Google's strategy of releasing early and often is also a brilliant and inventive marketing strategy: It dissuades potential competitors, raises the cost of entry to the market, and keeps users in Google's sphere of influence.

An Innovation Machine That Pays Off

In fact, contrary to popular belief, innovation isn't synonymous with profitability. Numerous researchers have demonstrated that the most innovative companies aren't necessarily the most profitable. Peter Drucker, the celebrated management guru, expounded on this at length in a 1996 interview: "The computer industry hasn't made a dime. . . . Intel and Microsoft make money, but look at all the people who are losing money all the world over. It is doubtful the industry has yet broken even."[5] Several studies since then have confirmed Drucker's pessimistic view that the most innovative business sectors are not inevitably those earning the most.[*]

Two phenomena explain this paradox. One is competition, which initially causes competitors to copy innovations very quickly. I've already discussed the diminishing window of time available for a company to profit from a new technology's competitive advantage. If a company wants to recoup its investment in R&D, it needs to take full advantage of this competitive edge during the first few months of a product's release. Traditionally, this means making massive marketing investments, creating a brand, and preparing a sales network for the rollout. All these propositions are very expensive. But Google's rollout strategy eliminates these traditional necessities: They get users to play with beta products and then test and promote them.

The second phenomena is the "diversion" of most benefits ultimately derived from a new product, sometimes called *the ripple effect*. Economists who study these issues have demonstrated that more than 80 percent of benefits go to parties other than the inventors.[6] To cite only one historical example, the public at large and other companies realized infinitely more benefits from the invention of electrical power and its distribution than the companies directly involved in its production. This is simply because entire new industries were developed to exploit the advantages afforded by electricity—household appliances and every other kind of electrical device. Nobody would complain about that, except perhaps those who originally invested in the invention of the processes to generate and distribute electricity.

---

* See, for example, Sarv Devaraj and Rajiv Kohli, *The IT Payoff: Measuring the Business Value of Information Technology Investments* (New York: Prentice Hall, 2002).

Google, however, has devised a mechanism that captures more of the benefits from its new products. It has two elements:

The sale of advertising on both its search engine and the sites visited through AdWords links (which contain more AdSense links) This allows Google to profit not only from its own in-house R&D but also from the efforts of all the companies that specialize in traffic optimization, companies whose sole task is to help site owners attract more visitors.

The assistance of other innovators When Google has acquired companies (a frequent occurrence), they haven't buried their technology or done it simply to make up for lost time but to bring the company's platform, their technology, reputation, and users into a larger service environment that the acquired company's engineers didn't develop.

Google is first to benefit from a rise in traffic that would otherwise divert profits elsewhere.

Just as a magnet attracts iron filings, Google attracts creative people and new ideas that, in another context, would be developed and deployed far from its search engine. Thus, it prevents many of the benefits of its own innovations from being diverted. By attracting innovation in this way, Google has been able to insulate itself from competition, speed up its development rate, and, day by day, make it a little more expensive for new competitors to stay in the race.

8

LIKE A SWISS ARMY KNIFE

I think Google should be like a Swiss Army knife: clean, simple, the tool you want to take everywhere. When you need a certain tool, you can pull these lovely doodads out of it and get what you want. So on Google, rather than showing you upfront that we can do all these things, we give you tips to encourage you to do things these ways. We get you to put your query in the search field, rather than have all these links up front. That's worked well for us. Like when you see a knife with all 681 functions opened up, you're terrified. That's how other sites are—you're scared to use them. Google has that same level of complexity, but we have a simple and functional interface on it, like the Swiss Army knife closed.[1]

—Marissa Mayer, former Google Product Manager (now Vice President, Search Products and User Experience) in a 2002 interview

Marissa Mayer's quote, comparing Google to a Swiss Army knife, perfectly describes one of the main driving forces of Google's success: the company's ability to introduce new offerings continually without messing up its existing ones. Now, let's see why this capacity is so important.

Earlier Product Strategies

Before we dig deeper into Google's strategy for product development, let's take a step back to Henry Ford's development of the standardized Model T automobile. Built on an assembly line and sold at relatively low prices to many people who had never owned a car, the Model T created a mass market for automobiles. But, at the same time, the car eliminated the expression of individuality and the exclusivity that had previously characterized the automobile purchase. The Model T was so standardized that your Model T looked just like the one parked down the street or around the corner.

As the automobile industry developed, options and accessories were offered to consumers to make their mass-produced car more unique. Manufacturers offered vehicles that could be customized with different paint colors, interior fittings, power trains, stereos, and so on, all according to the individual's preference.

This à la carte approach to product differentiation has been applied by product managers (like Marissa Mayer) to fields ranging from household appliances to hot dogs to hamburger toppings. Consumers in Western nations and in many Westernized nations are used to personalizing their purchases and have come to expect it.

But, on the other side, customization introduces logistical complications, burdens sales outlets, and increases the number of products rejected by consumers as either not being unique enough or being unique in the wrong way. This, in turn, increases product sales and development costs.

Consider Microsoft

Microsoft is a good example of the next phase of product development. Taking into account the ongoing decline in prices (according to the famous Moore's Law[*]), Bill Gates offered a range of products that would do whatever you wanted as long as you had a keyboard. Microsoft Office is often called *bloatware*; Office is the Model T of the workplace but fully loaded with accessories you didn't order. It contains not only word processing and spreadsheet applications but also many functions that nobody will ever fully utilize. Those functions are there (somewhere) if you can find them, but most people don't even know they exist.

Microsoft has caught plenty of flak from its critics for its approach to product development. Why include so many arcane features that only clog up menus, hog memory, and baffle new users? When competing software had fewer features, however, why would a consumer *not* opt for the product with so many extras for about the same price? Because more features make a product *seem* better. Microsoft's development of bloatware has actually given it a competitive advantage.

This strategy worked beautifully for Microsoft, initially contributing to its near-monopoly on office productivity software. But the addition of so many new features, and the increasing complexity of that software, has brought disadvantages, too. Every time Microsoft wants to upgrade its software, its engineers, in order to maintain "backward compatibility," have to make sure their enhancements are compatible with earlier releases and that everything still works, including the 200 new features they've just added. The richer the product is in features, the greater chance of incompatibility with earlier versions or of new bugs being introduced. And the issues become more complex and harder to control with each new version.

Microsoft has marketed itself into quite a bind. Rather than risk customer dissatisfaction by offering fewer features with each release or, more dramatically, simplifying their bloatware, the company is forced to increase the length of test periods and delay the release of new products, which is probably why its Office suite releases are predictably behind schedule.

---

[*] Gordon Moore, one of the founders of Intel, stated that the density of semiconductors doubled every 18 months, thus driving down technology prices proportionately.

The Google Swiss Army Knife

Google's Swiss Army knife approach to product development solves many of the problems that plague other product strategies. For one thing, every Google tool (or application) can be used autonomously—separate from other Google applications. If you really like Google Maps, for example, but you don't like Google Documents, you can just use Google Maps. That's not to say you can't use one Google tool with another, but the idea so far has been that you don't need to use tools together.

Unlike Microsoft's Office suite, Google tools go through separate development cycles and are released incrementally as features are ready. The release of a new version of Gmail, for example, doesn't replace the Gmail that you're already using, it enriches it. Also, if Google wants to modify one tool, that modification won't necessarily affect its other tools. A customer who has spent time learning a Google product doesn't lose any of his or her investment; the application simply changes incrementally.

When comparing Google's product development and release with that of Microsoft's, you can see a clear paradigm shift. Much of Google's success is a byproduct of the fact that most of Google's applications are delivered in real time, whether through a web browser or a telephone. You can't buy Google's applications in big box stores; you simply point your web browser to them and they're ready to be used. Or you can download and use them.

In contrast, the bulk of Microsoft's product line is sold through retail channels or preinstalled by computer manufacturers. As the major player in the traditional software market, each new version of Microsoft software requires a significant investment. Because Microsoft's investment is so great and the push behind each new product release so massive, Microsoft manages this expense by increasing the intervals between releases, adding new features in an attempt to justify the upgrade cost, and potentially frustrating customers who are inclined to resist having to learn something so dramatically new.

Google, on the other hand, has a much easier time with product development than a traditional software publisher. Changes to Google's software are typically discrete enhancements to applications with a relatively small feature set. These limited tools are inherently easier and cheaper to develop, test, and maintain than bloatware like Microsoft Office. The reduced complexity of Google's applications also reduces maintenance costs, which typically average 40 percent of an application's cost application during its lifecycle. (These costs include fixing bugs, preparing new versions, and user testing—costs that affect the life of a product between major releases.)

Google's application development has another interesting aspect. While most buyers of traditional, packaged software will complain loudly if a company like Microsoft tries to sell them beta software, Google doesn't hesitate to release beta applications and label them as such. Most users continue using applications like Gmail, which, even as I write this in the spring of 2009, are still listed as beta. That *beta* label allows Google to get away with a lot by lowering user expectations while at the same time delivering more than users might expect—for free.

Finally, Google's Swiss Army knife approach to tool development allows it to reinvent relationships with its users, who can choose the tools they want to use. Google doesn't impose anything on anybody; it's all about customization and individuality. Users design their own search portal with iGoogle, create their own maps with My Maps, customize the news stories displayed on Google News, and so on. Google is software your way; though, of course, within Google's parameters.

Is Google Lacking Direction?

Google's modular approach to tool development is sometimes misunderstood. The multiplicity of new tools often gives the impression that the company is lacking clear direction, that its leaders have no clear strategy. In fact, Google's roster of offerings has evolved along two parallel tracks: search tools and productivity tools. The tracks are complementary and share the common goal of making Google your Internet operating system.

Google makes no secret of wanting to remain the king of search. In its effort to do so, it continually releases applications offering personalized search tools as well as search tools designed to meet specific needs, such as sales (Shopping), information (News), academic research (Scholar), films and music (Video and Music), literary (Book Search), local information (Local), and so on.

Google's other significant track, which isn't as apparent, is represented by its efforts to release productivity tools that take aim squarely at Microsoft Office, the dominant Windows operating system, and user desktops in general. Google wants to own search, and it also wants to own your desktop by making Google the foundation of an Internet workstation, whether through offering tools to enable communication (Gmail, Groups, Orkut, Blogger, and so on), document production and distribution, or office collaboration (Calendar and Desktop Search)—tools designed so you can interact with everything on your computer via Google. And the list goes on and on.

The Online Swiss Army Knife: An Internet Operating System

The Swiss Army knife is a good metaphor for the way Google develops and deploys its products. It also aptly describes the growing collection of free tools the company makes available that help users with office productivity (Documents), keeping track of meetings and appointments (Calendar), instant messaging (Gmail), image and blogging software and hosting (Blogger), news with automatic alerts (News), and translation (Translate). And more is always on the way, of course.

Taken as a whole, you can see how Google is trying to develop an Internet operating system—one that runs through a web browser on any platform.

No matter the Google application, they all share the same style and feel whether they're running on Windows, Mac OS, Linux, or a cell phone. Because most Google tools run in a web browser, they are cross-platform, cross-browser applications. You can use most Google applications on any computer and on many mobile devices including phones, in just about any configuration and with few limitations.

Most Google applications offer a collaborative component, too, that allows more than one person to share the same document, map, video, and so on. Google encourages this collaboration (and builds its user base) by encouraging users to invite other people to try tools like Gmail (initially by invitation only) or to share a common calendar.

Ultimately, web applications release users from the constraints of fixed workstations, disks, and USB keys, allowing them to become truly mobile and social. Any Internet café will do.

You can easily imagine a whole new family of web-based applications just over the horizon. Many will certainly come from Google's development teams, but many more will come from other developers and users. Take Google Maps, for example. As of this writing, users have invented several new applications based on Google Maps, including ones that track gas prices, earthquakes, eBay listings, and YouTube postings. The list is endless. Microsoft has followed a similar model with its operating systems by working with developers to create DOS or certified Windows-based applications and by licensing its OS to almost anyone who would pay. Google, of course, is not seeking payment for its tools, but the effect is similar: Google's growing dominance in search and the further development of what you might call an *Internet operating system*.

What has made Microsoft so successful could make Google equally successful by reinforcing its dominant position in the search engine market. You can imagine Google becoming the equivalent of an operating system that serves as the basis for an environment or ecosystem of applications designed to help make better use of the huge mass of information available.

Google's Swiss Army knife could become to the Internet what the operating system is to the PC: a cornerstone impossible to circumvent, which, in turn, would make the company that controls it the king of the Internet.

9

FOR THE LOVE OF MATH AND MEASUREMENT

We're very analytical. We measure everything, and we sys-
tematized every aspect of what's happening in the company.
For example, we introduced a spreadsheet product this week.
I've already received my hourly updates on the number of
people who came in to apply to use the spreadsheet, the
number of people who are actually using it, the size of the
spreadsheets.[1]

—Eric Schmidt

Everyone who meets Sergey Brin notices his aptitude
as a mathematician. He has confidence in figures.
    Math is everywhere at Google: in pricing policy,
in discussions among engineers, in decisions about

whether to develop a new product, in the development of those products, in recruiting, and in evaluating employee performance. Google measures and analyzes everything.

This complicity between mathematics and management is nothing new. At the beginning of the industrial revolution, the mathematician Baron de Prony spent years compiling logarithmic tables that filled 19 folio volumes.[2] His work inspired the French and British theories of management and, during the 19th century, led to employees without mathematical training using the abacus so they would be able to calculate prices.

The theory of rational pricing, introduced by Jules Dupuit and Clément Colson, was further developed in the 1950s by economists and mathematicians like Maurice Allais, who applied it to the pricing of electricity. These methods all attempted to "achieve the maximum return on goods"* by defining a correct price, meaning a price that corresponded to the usefulness the purchaser received. Later, in the 1960s, engineers working on operational research applied mathematical calculation to problems that were considered too complex to manage, such as delivery and production schedules.

The methods Google uses to charge for Internet advertising fit precisely within this tradition. But as good engineers, the leaders of Google didn't stop there. They put computing power at the daily service of management in a number of ways.

The abundance of numerical data available at Google impresses every newcomer. Moma, the house intranet, can reportedly be used to track a multitude of numerical indicators and statistics. Employees can track clicks on AdWords and traffic statistics, the most frequently used search terms, the number of simultaneous searches, and much more. (Moma even includes information on the status of products in development and the number of employees on staff at any given time.) Once the data has been collected, users can employ one of the many statistical tools available to analyze the data they've collected.

---

* This expression was used by the economist Clément Colson at the end of the 19th century to describe railroad freight tariffs. Colson was a student of the original French engineer-economist, Jules Dupuit (1801–1866), who demonstrated that a monopoly will not conflict with the public interest if it sets the price of services according to their importance to the user. This concept was the basis for rational pricing of railroad fares and public utilities.

As a company created by computer scientists trained in the discipline of math, Google clearly sees statistical measurement, or *metrics*, as highly important. User behaviors are continually scanned, analyzed, and applied.

Real-Time Data Analysis

The direct data collected by Google's servers in real time is infinitely more reliable than the results of traditional research and market surveys. Extracting behavior models has replaced the traditional cycle of studies that rely on establishing assumptions and designing investigation protocols, surveys, and results analysis.

Not only is real-time market research a more precise way to measure user behavior, but this research is also far less expensive than traditional studies, offering results that can be used immediately. When you can graph real-time data and use it to predict behaviors, you don't have to rely on intuition as much.

In addition, because Google processes so much data, the company can narrowly segment user demographics and discover niches that would be invisible with smaller samples. (A small or invisible correlation on a sample of a few thousand people can become significant with a sample of several hundred thousand.)

Numbers Are Key

Google's virtually compulsive hunger for quantitative information puts it at the vanguard of a movement shared by companies like the fashion houses ZARA and H&M, the steel conglomerate Mittal, and the consumer goods giant Procter & Gamble. By processing real-time customer data quickly and acting accordingly, these companies are able to adjust their production schedules and marketing activities rapidly.

But differences exist among these companies. First, Google's massive use of data is not centralized as it is at a company like Mittal, where plant managers present the head of the company with a total of 66 technical reports (including fuel consumption, specific turn-around times measured in minutes, and so on). Centralization allows top management to practice ongoing performance benchmarking.[3]

With Google's decentralized approach, information is distributed broadly within the company: Its many intranet-based analytical tools make analyzing and interpreting data easy.

Second, at Google the use of quantitative analyses is not hindered by lack of technical expertise as it is at other companies.

According to Thomas Davenport, writing in the *Harvard Business Review*, "Analytical talent may be to the early 2000s what programming talent was to the late 1990s. Unfortunately, the US and European labor markets aren't exactly teeming with analytically sophisticated job candidates. Some organizations cope by contracting work to countries such as India, home to many statistical experts."[4]

This reliance on mathematics is one of Google's hallmarks. Few companies use as much math in their customer relationship vocabulary. Placing an advertisement on AdWords or AdSense is a lesson in how to quantify and interpret statistical data. For those who associate advertising with creativity, the focus on mathematics is a leap into a new universe.

This taste for mathematics is not limited to the collection and analysis of quantitative data, however. Where others might look for

---

Hiring: Measurement to the Rescue

Psychologists have long used math to evaluate people and measure cognitive abilities, attitudes, and personality traits. They typically use tests with questions that may seem odd or banal. But behind these questions, you usually find sophisticated techniques borrowed from mathematics and statistics, including *factor analysis* (describing variability among variables), *multidimensional scaling* (exploring similarities in data), data clustering, and *structural equation modeling* (testing causal relationships).

These techniques have not been lost on Google. For example, in 2006, its HR department asked all employees who had been working in the company for at least five months to fill out a 300-question survey. The data collected were compared with 25 measures of each employee's performance (which shows that performance is very carefully monitored). The aim was to find predictors of performance and adaptation to the company's very special culture.

This survey is now used to select the best candidates from among the more than 100,000 people who submit job applications to Google every month.

---

a Band-Aid solution, Google engineers use formulas to see the speed and contour of a problem. Their mathematical culture leads them to search for the general principle behind individual user behavior. This culture allows the engineers not only to apply solutions but also to interest the scientific community in problems and mobilize outsiders in the search for solutions. Spam and click fraud (more on this in Chapter 15) are two good examples. What might be seen only as technical problems of quality or safety at many companies become projects for outside researchers who contribute their expertise in the service of the company.

Mathematics and Management

Mathematics also directly affects Google's management methods. The practice of reasoning encourages precision. Mathematicians know the problems of approximation that are encountered in everyday life, but they discuss these problems with discipline.

"To speak with rigor about what is approximate"[5] is one definition of math that applies to Google's management practices. Nothing moves forward that isn't backed up by data or can't be proven. This sometimes gives meetings a hard edge (an opinion had better be provable, or it's likely to be disputed and attacked), but this rigor avoids smokescreens and most errors of logic such as the very classical confusion between volume and duration. (This confusion is exemplified by a very old question: Is the increased prison population really due to higher crime rates, or is it caused by longer sentences?) This pervasive scientific reasoning affects the atmosphere at Google, motivating employees. What better motivation than the desire to find a solution to a long-unsolved problem?

But this rigor can also breed arrogance, which is less a psychological factor than the natural result of a quasi-imperialistic view of truth. "Any mathematician, in everyday life, never stops speaking about truth and falsehood; what interests him is finding out what is true," explains Laurent Lafforgue, a renowned theorist in contemporary mathematics, who adds, "In mathematics, once a theorem is presented, it is there forever."[6]

When Math Is Used to Solve Problems
Related to Language

Google doesn't just exploit commercial information; it also applies mathematics to improve the performance of the Internet. This application involves one of the most advanced areas of research, *data mining*—the field originally chosen by Sergey Brin.[*]

In 1995, he published an article showing how mathematics could contribute to the usefulness of information related to literary analysis as well as equations.[7] The article, written with two Stanford professors, addresses plagiarism. The idea is quite simple: When an author publishes a book, he or she loads the text into a "copy detection server" that slices it into a multitude of fragments as sentences are tagged and classified in a huge digital library. Each time a new work is published, the work is compared with what is already in the database. Two documents showing a relatively high percentage of similarity (how much is not specified) indicates possible plagiarism, which a human reader can then check. This has a certain irony, considering Google's copyright problems.[†]

A similar mechanism is used in spelling and grammar checkers and particularly in machine translation. Language differences constitute a subject that is both extremely difficult and crucial for further development of the Internet. Language barriers create immense gray areas and make thousands of relevant pages unavailable to users. Current solutions to machine translation are pretty primitive. All you need to do is translate any text from a foreign language with one of the available programs and then retranslate it back into the source language to

---

[*] Another data-mining specialist at Google is Udi Manber, the author of Sif, a file analysis program. Manber became a manager in Google's engineering department after having worked at Yahoo! and Amazon.com. He wrote another program to identify similarities among sequences in Java programs, thus helping to eliminate redundancies that unnecessarily complicate code. This program has implications for plagiarism detection and other data-mining applications.

[†] Google has been taken to court several times for copyright infringement—for example, alleged violation of publishers' copyright (Google Book Search) and YouTube's hosting of copyrighted videos or songs.

see how far these solutions have to go. Google's web page translation feature delivers readable, if clunky, results for pairs of similar languages but near-gibberish for some other combinations.

In considering these issues, Brin, his co-authors, and everyone else interested in these questions are dealing with problems not encountered in traditional structured databases that use only data specified in advance. A name, a date of birth, or a sales total is defined as an *object* (identity type) and also by its *form* (the numbers or characters contained in the entry). But text in a normal document doesn't work this way. Automated analysis will require answers to the following questions:

- How can text be automatically separated ("chopped," in the authors' terminology) into relevant units? This separation can be done only by recognizing material elements such as punctuation marks and blank spaces. Yet separating a block of text into sentences is a complex process because the period that the human eye sees as marking the end of a sentence is also used to separate letters in abbreviations like "U.S."

- What are the relevant units (specialized vocabulary terms that will vary in length) for the task at hand? These will differ depending on whether the goal is to detect plagiarism, translate languages, or suggest optional synonyms or syntax within the same language.

- Which units will be most efficient, given the dual constraints of machine capacity and speed?

Finding answers to these apparently simple questions requires the development of complex, extremely powerful algorithms. As only one example, the tests described previously using the plagiarism detection engine found a significant *noise level* of coincidental verbatim repetitions (0.6 percent, or the equivalent of two to three sentences per paper) in articles on totally unrelated subjects. Thus, the solution did not reach the level of sophisticated analysis.

10

KEEP THE TEAMS SMALL

One of the most common principles of management theory since at least Henri Fayol[*] says that a hierarchical structure can only be truly effective with one manager for a maximum of seven employees.[†] Beyond that, control is lost, and quality and productivity decline. As explained by proponents

---

[*] Henri Fayol (1841–1925), a French management theorist, was a key figure in the turn-of-the-century Classical School of management theory. He is considered by many to be the father of modern operational management theory.

[†] This thesis was redeveloped more recently under the term *span of control*. The later work arrives at the same conclusions Fayol did on the day before the First World War.

of the *span of control theory*, developed by Sir Ian Hamilton in 1922, managers have a finite amount of time, energy, and attention to devote to their job. To quote Hamilton, "The nearer we approach the supreme head of the whole organization, the more we ought to work towards groups of three; the closer we get to the foot of the whole organization, the more we work towards groups of six."[1]

This ratio of 1 manager per 7 subordinates is applied just about everywhere. According to the *Statistical Abstract of the United States: 2004–2005*, about 1 in 10 employees in the United States is a manager, and the ratio is not much different in other countries. (In France, the estimate is 1 manager for every 7.5 workers.)

This principle applies most everywhere it seems, except at Google. For example, at the end of 2005, the company had 1 manager for every 20 employees; a year before, you would commonly see a single manager supervising more than 40 people.

Was this a mistake of youthful inexperience? Or perhaps a delusion of idealists who knew nothing about effective management? Perhaps a deficit caused by fast growth? All of those criticisms were voiced, but wrongly. This extremely light structure, short on managers, results from the desire to create a company that is innovative, nimble, responsive, and fast on its feet.

Fight the Bureaucracy

Larry Page, Sergey Brin, and Marissa Mayer discovered the world of business when the conventional wisdom among managers was "downsizing is the solution." They heard plenty of criticism of the bureaucracy within large companies and surely observed previous disasters in Silicon Valley. They knew, too, that many once-powerful companies had choked to death on what John Kenneth Galbraith, in his book *The New Industrial State*, called their *technostructure*—the influential management cliques inside a large company that control economic decisions.[2]

But even if they had not studied management texts, Google's original core group would have known that a light infrastructure would reduce costs, distribute payroll more equitably, avoid bureaucratic trends, and inhibit the natural propensity of managers to hire too many people. But knowing that it is better to build an organization that can function with a light management framework is one thing; doing it is another.

Of course, criticizing the technostructure is easy, but it does perform some needed functions. Among its benefits, the technostructure ensures coordination, organizes and controls workflow, and offers a way to communicate instructions, objectives, and information throughout the organization. When you reduce the technostructure, you need to replace it with something. Google has chosen to replace much of that technostructure with technology itself and small teams.

The economic model that Brin and Page chose simplified the task. Cutting out the cost of ad sales through automated bidding reduced all the costs related to sales as well as the overhead needed for contacts and conversations with customers. Publicity, marketing, sales initiatives, in-house price discussions, and price negotiations with customers all consume time and contribute to bureaucracy's growth. Google has reduced many of these costs, but this cost reduction is only a part of the story.

Small Teams Facilitate Innovation

Google's structure is so light because Brin and Page wanted to reduce the coordination and administrative costs that hamper engineers and reduce the time devoted to innovation. Time spent reading and writing proposals, negotiating, explaining choices, ensuring instructions are understood and followed, and enforcing policies is time taken away from inventing.

Google accomplishes this feat using several parameters simultaneously. I've already discussed one innovation, the 20 percent rule for personal projects. But another important innovation is Google's use of small, autonomous teams.

Google certainly didn't invent the concept of small teams. The group that developed the first Apple Macintosh consisted of no more than five people—at the beginning. Bill Gates has often sung the praises of small teams (which is not to say that he succeeded in imposing them at Microsoft). And well before those innovators, several authors warned companies against using large teams. But even if many people know the virtues of small teams, few know how to make full use of them and are able to resist the propensity of teams to grow.

Google's stroke of genius comes in assigning projects with limited objectives and short deadlines that are seldom longer than six weeks. Google executives say this organizational model, which puts stringent constraints on performance and time, was implemented because it allows numerous projects to be developed simultaneously, and it results in more invention. Google can roll out new releases within short intervals because hundreds of projects are completed using only a few thousand engineers.

But the model has other advantages. For one, small teams improve productivity and efficiency. By limiting teams to a maximum of six people, the company must subdivide projects into units that a small group can complete. In practice, this requires precisely defined goals and easily monitored deadlines, which equates to managing by objective. Set the goal and your employees work to reach it. The idea is simple enough: You'll get better results from a team if you first define what you want the team members to accomplish.

Because projects are short in duration, deadlines are easy to track, and problems appear quickly, which means they can be solved quickly. Small teams also help projects move fast—a key to success on the Internet. Daily pressure to achieve short-term goals is strong, and peer pressure to focus on the task at hand is a potent force. Take it from Jeff Bezos, founder of Amazon.com. When a *Wall Street Journal* reporter asked Bezos for the secret to his success, he replied, "To work quickly and correct the small errors later. The only fatal error on the Web is to be too slow."[3]

Small Teams Are Efficient

Because small teams are ill equipped to win political battles for additional resources, their members tend to eschew hallway politics and seek technical solutions instead. In order to advance their project, team members stick to norms, use available modules, and generally work in more efficient ways.

Even in a company as rich as Google, the resources available to small teams are inevitably limited; they have to make do with what is quickly and easily procurable. After all, why reinvent the wheel when resources are scarce? Why not just use the wheel and put your efforts elsewhere? And Google is not hesitant to use existing tools—such as open source databases or the Linux operating system—when those tools meet its needs. If a program is suitable, Google will adapt it to house standards rather than rewrite it from scratch.

Small teams also prevent freeloading and can reduce conflicts: Each member's performance is easily observed, and peer pressure ensures that everyone pulls his weight. When deadlines are looming, employees tempted to shirk their responsibilities are quickly detected and castigated, leaving little time for political nonsense.

Small teams force their members to be creative because a boss isn't present to give specific instructions on how to do things. They also give rise to a certain versatility. People in charge of very large projects must divide work and delegate tasks to subordinates, who tend to create further bureaucracy, including their own management committee, organizational chart, and other departmental functions like human resources, communications, and finance.

It's Not Just the Size

By reducing the need for controls and giving employees more autonomy, small teams with precise objectives and deadlines can dramatically reduce the need for management oversight and facilitate the construction of flat organizations. But this is not all.

Google uses teams of three to six people. This number is a good one if you take Jeff Bezos's word for it: "To the degree that you can get people in a team small enough that they can be fed on two pizzas, you'll get a lot more productivity. About six people is a good size. But it depends on how hungry the people are."[4]

According to three German researchers who studied the performance of a variety of companies around Cologne, Germany, the optimum workgroup size is three people. As soon as the group exceeds four people, effectiveness (measured by weekly hours worked by each member) starts to decline, as shown in the following figure.[5]

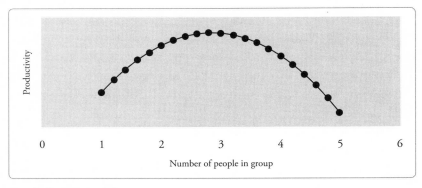

Graph of optimum workgroup size

Size is obviously important, but simply creating small teams is not enough. From what is known about Google's methods, management plays a key role in making sure everything functions perfectly.

The composition of the team is one key to its success. The better qualified a team's members, the better the team will function. In companies that have undergone the transition from a traditional to team-based structure, the more qualified people spontaneously gravitate toward the team approach where more personal responsibility is required.

A certain level of heterogeneity in expertise improves team performance because the people who work together complement each other as they observe and learn from fellow team members. The rate of turnover is also crucial: Small teams should be short-lived in order to fight the development of bureaucracy.

Finally, consider the work environment and the company's organization. Small teams are effective at Google because internal communication keeps everyone up to speed on the progress of individual projects. Competition among teams, or at least the possibility of comparison, improves productivity, too, as shown by several lab studies.[6]

The idea of small teams is not new. If they appear to be more effective and durable at Google, it's because the company has developed a particular cultural environment that supports small teams and encourages their development.

11

COORDINATION THROUGH TECHNOLOGY

In order to be effective, small teams need a special ecology. Google created one by mobilizing technology to solve the biggest problem of any business: that of coordinating people and their responsibilities. But the company didn't stop at giving all its employees a powerful computer system with leading-edge applications. Google built an organization that enables people to share ideas and project specifications quickly.

People who want to work together have many ways to coordinate. Within a corporation, management generally determines how coordination happens. Managers oversee the work of their employees and coordinate efforts by dividing work and distributing it sequentially: Each step in product development is a cog in the industrial assembly line immortalized by Charlie Chaplin in his film *Modern Times*.

But other types of coordination do exist. The influential sociologist James D. Thompson, founding editor of Cornell's *Administrative Science Quarterly*, identified three modes of coordination in his work *Organizations in Action*:[1] sequential, reciprocal, and community, also called, respectively, coordination, cooperation, and collaboration. They are defined as follows:

- *Sequential mode* is based on the traditional corporate hierarchy: Employees are given specific tasks and are supervised to make sure they follow directions.

- *Reciprocal mode* is based on constant interactions among participants. For example, Thompson describes the traditional relationship between a physician and a nurse. The nurse prepares the patient for the physician; the physician completes his or her task; then the doctor returns the patient to the nurse.

- *Community mode* is based on autonomous players' sharing common resources. Thompson's example in this instance is that of teachers in schools. Teachers work individually in their own classes, but they share classrooms, the library, and administrative services.

Google adapted the last of these models, community or collaborative mode, to industrial engineering. Whether they did so as a result of reading Thompson I cannot say. What seems clear, though, is that they adopted the organizational model they knew best—that of the university.

At first glance, using the field of education as a model for building an effective, dynamic business may seem strange, yet the academic model has some interesting characteristics. First, it functions with a weak hierarchical structure: In the case of a large institution, one chancellor or president and a small board of regents enable the university to function with thousands of students and hundreds of professors.

Second, an educational institution also allows its employees (the faculty) a high degree of autonomy. Their work is guided by curricula (universities in Boston, Los Angeles, London, and New Delhi use many of the same textbooks), and faculty require little daily supervision. Criticism from students and their parents checks those who stray from the program, thus ensuring a relatively high degree of conformity. By taking inspiration from academia and following a collaborative model (whether they call it that or something similar), Google has limited coordination overhead and standardized common resources like databases and data processing languages.

The Technology of Shared Information

For those who might be put off by this praise of the university model, I'll add that Page, Brin, and Schmidt did not simply replicate this model without modifying it. They adapted, adding technology to equip their staff with sophisticated coordination tools.

At first, Google used existing groupware, or *Computer Supported Cooperative Work* (*CSCW*), a term first coined by Irene Greif and Paul M. Cashman in 1984 to describe a collaborative work environment that can be supported by computer systems. CSCW software or groupware contains four types of tools: communication (email and videoconferencing); systems for sharing applications, files, or documents (collaborative editing systems and forums); search engines to find information quickly; and automated workflow management. For example, at most companies a vacation request must be approved by an employee's boss and then by human resources. Workflow software automates the transfer of the request and may also trigger a check of the employee's accumulated vacation time. Once approvals are in order, the employee is notified. Human intervention is required only if a problem arises.

The real development and deployment of collaborative workplace tools began with the emergence of personal computers. One of the pioneers of these tools, Terry Winograd, was Larry Page's professor at Stanford and went on to become a Google consultant. In the 1980s, Winograd worked with Douglas Engelbart, Harvey Lethman, and others studying work automation.[2] Many companies today use collaborative software that resulted from Winograd, Engelbart, and Lethman's research. What sets Google apart is that its management team apparently had no doubt whatsoever about the value of using these tools. They didn't do a trial run to see if the software was viable; they simply adopted it from the get-go.

Moma: Abundant Information

Before Google went public and regulations required more confidentiality, employees could find everything about Google on the company intranet, affectionately named *Moma* by its users. No one really knows where the nickname originated, but one theory is it refers both to a maternal image and New York City's Museum of Modern Art (MoMA), which is renowned for its large collection of masterpieces and the creativity of its exhibitions.

Staff members connected to the intranet could find information about ad sales in real time (a good way to see how the company is doing), progress reports on various projects (which encouraged them to pitch in when one fell behind), and many other aspects of the company's daily business.

In every case, information on Moma is presented in a way that contributes to the company's betterment. One good example is the Google employee directory. Most directories found on corporate intranets are as tedious as the phone book: a name, an email address, and a phone number. Moma, however, also provides information on individuals' areas of expertise, describes their projects, and shows their employment status—information that would normally be considered confidential.

Rather than keep this information confidential, Google publishes it so everybody can use it. This changes employee behavior. Knowing coworkers' objectives, limitations, expertise, and specific projects discourages others from disturbing them needlessly. Bothering a fellow employee with questions that he or she doesn't have time to answer or probably can't answer is pointless. And, of course, publishing an employee's areas of expertise also encourages concern about his or her reputation so the employee can work on maintaining and improving it.

By widely distributing information in this manner, employees adjust their behavior to suit the company's needs *and* make best use of their colleagues' capabilities—without management intervening. This openness helps create what Friedrich Hayek[3] and Michael Polanyi[4] (familiar to many for his work on tacit knowledge and the effects of self-organization within companies) called *spontaneous order*: the spontaneous emergence of order out of seeming chaos. Critics could argue that an abundance of information may have a reverse effect. Everybody knowing (nearly) everything about everyone else creates a form of mutual control within the group that is more typical of a religious cult than a democratic society. No doubt that is a price to be paid for a more systematic use of personal information. However, no evidence exists that these tools have caused even the slightest negative reaction at Google. Perhaps because Google is a young company founded on innovation, coworkers are more interested in other people's accomplishments than their personal attributes. In addition, everyone at every level has confidence in the ability of technology to address social problems.

But are things so different in more traditional, hierarchical companies where information is segmented? Motivational seminars and other group activities that send workers to offsite events far from their family and intense work schedules that don't allow for a minute of spare time are also ways to adjust behavior.

Blogs at Work

By now we all know about blogs—those sources of instant news and personal opinion that took off with the advent of Blogger in 1999. In September 2003, when Google acquired Blogger, management immediately installed it on the company intranet. (At the time, Blogger was called B.I.G., referring not to "big brother" but to "Blogger In Google.") Biz Stone, one of the creators of Blogger and a subsequent co-founder of companies like Odeo and Twitter, describes the Google intranet in his book *Who Let the Blogs Out* as "one of the most amazingly vibrant and smart virtual playgrounds in the world."[5]

Soon, hundreds of Google employees had created personal blogs as well as professional ones dedicated to a project, an idea, or a market.

For instance, the blog for everyone who works on Blogger at Google allows those employees to track industry news, competition, and potential partners, as well as new developments, ideas, and projects.

Blogs are much more than online newsletters. They combine the functions of writing and publishing with creating social bonds. You can subscribe to a blog just as you can to a newspaper, except most blogs appeal to a specific community with similar interests. The blogs communicate information without management intervening, and information is passed among players from different departments without screening, bypassing divisions of labor, management, and organizational structure that simply become irrelevant.

Blogs don't disseminate information manufactured and controlled from above, as with traditional memos and first-generation knowledge-management tools. The information comes from coworkers at lower levels and is coordinated by whoever needs the information. By subscribing to a blog and commenting, people decide whether to collaborate with others. They can create their own activities of focus and feedback. Some blogs will become popular whereas others disappear. In practice, blogging communities can be established within a few days, weeks, or months and then fade away when the topics that gave rise to them lose importance.

The benefits of blogs to a business like Google are immediate. They translate into the following:

Time saved   Rather than attend seemingly interminable meetings where you listen to people talk about things that don't concern you or get involved with paperwork that has no practical value, employees can turn to blogs for the information they need, when they need it.

Concentrated information   The information on blogs is of high quality and depth. Information in a blog will be focused on the needs of a limited number of subscribers who consult the blog and comment when they have time.

Personal autonomy   Unlike earlier project-management software that automated procedures, blogs allow individuals who build their own blogging community to set their own rules.

In the opinion of sociologists and other consultants, the fact that the earlier tools did not allow this autonomy is why they failed in other organizations.

With these tools, coordination among teams escapes management scrutiny. This isn't to say use of these tools amounts to anarchy—far from it, even though things may look that way to outsiders. Google employees have voluntarily placed themselves within a control-and-correction mechanism that is based not only on personal fame and reputation but also on the vigilance of coworkers who are not at all shy about correcting errors.

Instead of a formal corporate organization mapped by flowcharts, Google relies on its social fabric, one that comprises networks of confidence that arise spontaneously among employees. Organizational theorists ignored these factors for a long time, as well as the work of sociologists and ethnologists. At Google, these ideas are displayed everywhere. With these tools, special-interest communities establish themselves within the company. These transitory communities develop values and criteria for judgment, build individual fame and reputation, and introduce control mechanisms for individual activity. They are more informal than those typically used by management but possibly more stringent. One former employee described leaving the company because he didn't feel he was up to the job. His impression that he wasn't meeting expectations led him to decide it was time to go.

All companies contain abstract communities built around many different criteria: age, seniority, level of interaction in an office or workshop, job experience, education, or vocation. Some traditional managers consider these communities a threat to their own authority and view them with suspicion. At Google, to the contrary, these communities are equipped and mobilized.

A New Role for Management

All of this autonomy greatly modifies management's role. Things don't work the same in a company where coworkers are free to coordinate their own activities and in another where layers of managers insist on controlling everything. Supervising 20 to 30 people instead of

7 to 10 requires a different demeanor. Managing people is no longer a question of controlling their work down to the slightest detail.

Incapable of tracking the daily activities of his or her staff and forced to trust them, a manager who is under pressure from his or her own boss must move quickly. Even if he or she is talented, the manager won't have time for small talk. Individual conversations will be less frequent and inevitably shorter because time is limited. The manager has to place more importance on facts, figures, and measurable data. This requires a management style that is more rational than charismatic.

This topic comes up regularly in conversations with the leaders of companies operating in the new economy, not only at Google but also at Amazon.com. According to Jeff Bezos, founder of Amazon.com:

> For every leader in the company, not just for me, there are decisions that can be made by analysis. . . . These are the best kinds of decisions! They're fact-based decisions. The great thing about fact-based decisions is that they overrule the hierarchy. The most junior person in the company can win an argument with the most senior person with a fact-based decision. Unfortunately, there's this whole other set of decisions that you can't ultimately boil down to a math problem.[6]

These entrepreneurs reverse the traditional tendency in all companies to associate knowledge, truth, and position. Traditionally, the higher a person's position in the organization, the more he or she officially knows and the greater the chance that what he or she says is likely to be true—or at least to be considered so.

Saying that decisions should be based on facts is not, of course, original. What's original is these leaders' penchant for analytical reasoning and, perhaps more important, the types of data they use. They try as much as possible to work with real data, tangible figures, and meaningful samples. By using technology, they can find the facts; intuition and impulse give way to analysis.

By freeing the organization from a whole series of controls necessary in traditional companies, communication tools have allowed Google to grow without developing extensive systems of bureaucracy and technostructure. A manager cannot control more than six or seven people in a traditional organization because he or she has to supervise and control not only the relationships between himself or herself and each worker but also the relationships among all workers. Each time a new team member is added, the number of relationships that need to be supervised increases exponentially.

V.A. Graicunas, a consulting engineer who was the first to analyze this problem systematically, demonstrated that increasing a group from 4 to 5 members, and thereby improving its work capacity by 20 percent, would increase the number of relationships the group leader would need to supervise by 127 percent (which might also equal the increase in interpersonal problems).[7] This progression accelerates as additional staff are added, so much so that the task quickly exceeds the brainpower of even the most brilliant manager. For example, supervising 12 workers requires the manager to "track" 24,708 relationships. This result may seem odd at first, but this figure includes direct relationships (from a superior to a subordinate), cross relationships (from subordinate to subordinate), and group relationships (from superior to any combination of subordinates). The only conventional solution is to load up on technostructure and create more management positions. But these superimposed layers developed by management only breed more bureaucracy.

By equipping its workers with communication tools and letting staff coordinate itself through mutual interaction, Google has developed an organizational model that looks more like a rosette or star polygon than the traditional flowchart. In this model, wherein each person maintains relationships with everyone else, adding another team member increases the number of relationships that each person must manage by one unit. Thus, the cognitive limitations of managers are no longer an obstacle to growth. The company can increase its staffing quickly without also creating a heavy technostructure.

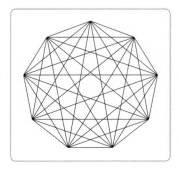

A star polygon

This model is, of course, only one possibility—but it is one that helps explain Google's rapid growth. Page and Brin invented the model, but they could have found inspiration in what Douglas Engelbart envisaged in 1992, when he wrote one of the first articles about using technology to facilitate coordination within companies.[8]

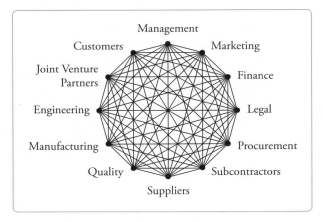

Knowledge domains of a manufacturing organization according to Douglas Engelbart

All of this greatly modifies management's role. At Google, employees have the means to coordinate freely. Unable to track the daily action of his or her subordinates, the manager must have confidence in his or her staff to accomplish the demand from higher management to complete projects quickly. Even with a very large staff, a manager has to get down to basics: upstream objectives and downstream results, which means fewer, and necessarily shorter, meetings.

Information Technology and the Organization

Over the past 30 years, organizational theory has borrowed heavily from several data processing models. The first computer systems, which were large mainframes, were used to centralize functions within a company, such as accounting and payroll. Until the end of the 1950s, large companies still had decentralized management staff, with regional authority for hiring, discipline, and wages. During the 1970s and 1980s, computers led to increased centralization at headquarters, putting the data processing department in charge of payroll. This movement coincided with an effort to standardize and rationalize corporate rules. The advent of minicomputers and then personal computers during the mid-1980s reversed the trend, decentralizing some of these functions, particularly the acquisition of data from the field.

During the 1990s, efforts were made to create companywide data processing systems for Enterprise Resource Planning (ERP). The goal was to consolidate and coordinate all applications and company data. This consolidation would—at least in theory—give leaders a panoramic view. These undertakings coincided with the development of complex dashboards (or information displays) that went far beyond the cost accounting systems devised at General Motors during the 1920s and used by executives of conglomerates throughout the 1960s.

Balance scorecards that associate and integrate financial, commercial, and human resources information illustrate this tendency. More recently, network data processing has been used as the basis for a theoretical model of how companies network with other companies. The influence of data processing has become even stronger as programmers automate functions with applications that have actually replaced many traditional analysis methods within organizations. The most recent methods like Business Process Reengineering (BPR) are directly inspired by this principle as voiced by BPR's creators Michael Hammer and James Champy: "Instead of embedding outdated processes in silicon and software, we should obliterate them and start over. We should 'reengineer' our businesses: use the power of modern information technology to radically redesign our business processes in order to achieve dramatic improvements in their performance."[9] This sentiment applies to both data processing methods and organizational structure, which are now merging in many ways. Google's management system further melds technological and organizational paradigms.

12

THE SECRET IS IN THE FACTORY

In a world where new products are copied as soon as they become popular, industrial successes are often related to production innovations. Consultant Michael Hammer, co-author of *Reengineering the Corporation: A Manifesto for Business Revolution*, calls these "operational innovations."[1]

Examples abound. Production principles are paramount in the just-in-time system responsible for Toyota's success. Dell Computer became a market leader in record time by offering its customers made-to-order computers. And Wal-Mart became the leading worldwide retailer by reducing inventory storage costs.

Google is in an entirely different line of business, but part of its success is due to its capacity to invent, or at least implement, a powerful production system that its competitors cannot copy, simply because this system is the company's best-kept secret.

A Limitation Becomes an Asset

Like many other aspects of Google's business venture, the devising of its production system was a matter of chance. When Page and Brin developed their search algorithm, they wanted to put the entire Internet on their computers. Theirs was an irrational but natural ambition: A search engine couldn't really satisfy its users unless those users could access every document available on the Internet, or at least as many as possible.

Page and Brin's ambition may have been unrealistic, what with so many obscure nooks and crannies on the Web, but that didn't matter. This ambition led them to consider from the beginning how to build a large-capacity computer system.

If Page and Brin had had more money, they surely would have bought one of the powerful server systems available from several manufacturers. But in 1998, a couple of college kids short on cash had to scrounge for whatever equipment they could find. Historians tell how they filled their office at Stanford and then their first workspace with machines that were begged, borrowed, donated, or bought on sale—a feat that would have been nearly impossible to accomplish only 15 years earlier, when computers were much more scarce and much more expensive. The fact that computers had effectively become commodities by the late 1990s dramatically lowered entry costs for these two entrepreneurs.

Redundancy

This limitation was an opportunity in disguise. Secondhand computers aren't necessarily in good working order, so they tend to break down frequently and unexpectedly. The solution to mitigating this defect is well known and obvious: redundancy. If you think one component might go down, you replicate the data on other components to decrease the risk of loss. Born of necessity, redundancy became a centerpiece of the factory Page and Brin would eventually build. (On a larger scale, redundancy has also allowed Google to safeguard against disasters by distributing its servers geographically. If an earthquake or a flood shuts down one server farm, servers in other locations will be able to pick up the load.)

Initially, the perceived need for redundancy presented problems, not least of which was where to put all that equipment. Here, historians tell how Larry Page began invading nearby offices, a tactic that didn't work for long for obvious reasons. Early on, he and Brin had to figure out a way to house all those computers within a small space. The simple solution was to use rack cabinets with casters that allowed them to be moved from place to place. You can easily see how important that was for maintaining continuity.

This limitation also caused Page and Brin to pay close attention to managing their computer network. Distributed data processing is a complex, highly technical, and difficult endeavor, all the more so when you're trying to patch together a network of PCs that weren't designed to be used in that way.

Here, too, Page and Brin did something unconventional; instead of entrusting the task to a networking specialist who might be limited by yesterday's techniques, they found Dr. Jim Reese, a neurosurgeon whose career included years in medical computer science. Reese's unconventional experience led him to explore and eventually merge ideas and concepts from computer science and neuroanatomy, a discipline that traditionally deals with network plasticity. He chose to build a system where computers are used for what they do best, repetitive tasks, and where the network quickly reconstructs itself.

Powerful Production Equipment

Lack of funds and lack of space helped the Google co-founders to build a unique, highly automated factory, using the latest means of distributed data processing. The entire Google network is based on a model for processing large data sets and dispatching tasks across a large cluster, using MapReduce and the Google File System.

MapReduce distributes tasks by running programs in parallel on a large cluster of commodity machines. The MapReduce system balances and manages program execution, allowing Google's programmers to utilize the resources of a large distributed system easily. According to Google, "a typical MapReduce computation processes many terabytes of data on thousands of machines."[2]

The *Google File System* (first known as *BigFiles*) is a scalable, distributed, high-performance file system designed to meet Google's file storage needs. The Google File System (or GFS) is a fault-tolerant system that runs on inexpensive commodity hardware. The largest GFS cluster as of this writing "provides hundreds of terabytes of storage across thousands of disks on over a thousand machines, and it is concurrently accessed by hundreds of clients."[3]

Taken as a whole, Map Reduce and GFS allow Google to do the following things:

Maintain data integrity   Data is copied and recopied to several machines, so it's unlikely to disappear. When a failure occurs on a particular machine, that machine is stopped and rebooted automatically. If the machine doesn't come back to life, machines with duplicate data make additional copies elsewhere. This ensures an almost zero likelihood of losing anything in the database.

Maintain network integrity   If part of the network goes down (for example, because of a natural disaster), or if the network is taken offline for maintenance, users are routed to other servers and can continue to use the service uninterrupted.

Facilitate maintenance and upgrades   With pages replicated on several different servers, any machine can easily be taken offline and upgraded. Users are automatically and transparently redirected to active machines.

Optimize production   Because tasks are distributed among several servers, they can be allotted according to the size and popularity of their pages. Massively parallel computing ensures that processors don't remain idle while awaiting data. The principle is similar to that in a workshop wherein everyone knows how to perform several tasks, so they can easily fill in for one another.

Reduce costs By reducing unutilized processing resources, Google gets more productivity from each machine, making them all more efficient and reducing costs by making continual adjustments to resources that match current needs. With large farms of small machines, Google avoids the "accordion effect" typically experienced by companies that rely on large, integrated systems: Because upgrades are costly and disruptive, they're postponed until the system slows to a crawl, at which point companies add more capacity than they need (hence the accordion name)—capacity that is wasted until demand catches up.

Google is said to have somewhere between 30 and 60 server farms, depending on whom you ask. The exact figure is confidential and probably changes regularly, but it is irrelevant anyway. What is more important is Google's ability to locate (or relocate) data centers geographically to minimize data transfer time. Long data transfer times are not a problem with textual data, but when serving large video files, transfer time can be an issue.

NOTE *The use of remotely distributed server farms also has political implications. For example, if the US government were to step up its domestic surveillance measures and choose to rummage through users' personal data stored on Google's servers, those servers could all be moved to a country whose government has a greater concern for personal privacy.*

Use Existing Infrastructure

Google's entire data factory is built on an extremely powerful software platform, utilizing many tens of thousands of computers (according to some estimates, as many as 450,000). This platform is surely one of Google's main strengths and its best protection against competition. Mobilizing an army of microcomputers takes money, but even with unlimited funds, quickly developing a system to manage all of those machines would be far more difficult. Google's ability to do so ensures high performance and makes all the difference. Computing power and software are mutually reinforced; the more data processed in a massively parallel architecture, the higher its efficiency.

Of course, Google could not have built all of this infrastructure without the benefit of a mature data processing industry: The microcomputers at the foundation of this formidable factory were—at least at the beginning—commodity products like your everyday office computer that cost no more than $1,000 each.

By all accounts, the system developed by Google's engineers could be described as technological cross-breeding. They were able to move as quickly as they did because they often needed only to borrow previous solutions for problems as they arose. Engineers borrowed heavily from traditional supercomputing techniques, especially for system management tasks, by using batch processing techniques developed for large systems. Other solutions came from experience with microcomputers, which achieved high performance slowly because of their limited processing power.

For example, the filter that allows you to search documents quickly is derived directly from technology used to optimize PC hard drives. Google's engineers also borrowed from relational database technology: Data from web pages is broken into independent units called *shards*, which are then stored redundantly on multiple *chunk servers*.

Borrowing ideas and solutions from existing technologies gave Google's engineers more time to answer unfamiliar questions and solve new problems, for instance how to build a scalable distributed file system? How to compare and duplicate computer files? How to automate all these operations and minimize their cost?

Finally, Google benefits from the recent surplus of data transmission network capacity. The United States has a lot of *dark fiber*, or unutilized optical cables.

In the 1990s, tech companies raced to modernize their networks, resulting in gross overcapacity. Because the cost of building infrastructure is higher than the cost of cables, companies overequipped their facilities in anticipation of future needs. While waiting until these resources are needed, these companies have chosen to rent out their idle capacity, allowing Google to negotiate long-term contracts that ensure high capacity at low prices.

At first, these rental agreements helped Google save costs by eliminating the need to buy long-haul transport services to interconnect data centers. In the long run, these agreements will enable Google to develop activities that consume more bandwidth quickly, like voice and video, and support new Internet standards that could prove to be the next IT frontier.

PART III

Put Users First; the Rest Will Follow

Like most companies, Google has a mission statement or "philosophy." Google's philosophy is divided into 10 points; each point is one sentence long. The first and most interesting is quoted in the title of this part of the book. Unlike most corporate mission statements, this phrase did not come about through long committee discussions: This statement is Larry Page's mantra. Early on, when people asked him about financing his projects, he always replied with something like, "Don't worry about it. If our users are satisfied, if we give them all they want and more, we'll be able to find some money." This sentiment should be emphasized because it is exactly the opposite of what business schools teach and management experts advise.

This concept is embedded in Google's corporate DNA. In their very first paper, Page and Brin criticized search engines that neglected users at the expense of advertisers. Looking through the company's history and seeing how many arguments have been made against advertising is amusing. In that first paper, Page and Brin analyzed the economic model of funding search through advertising and pointed out, "The goals of the advertising business model do not always correspond to providing quality search to users."[1] In fact, they stubbornly resisted all pressure to give in to the demands of the advertising industry. Much of their success was to come from this insistence on making Internet users their top priority. Since that first paper, the Internet has become an international cultural asset, and Google's leaders have been given a thousand reasons to change their mind. Would they have given in if they had been subjected to constant pressure from a powerful marketing department? Who knows. At any rate, they didn't, simply because they had the bright—and bold—idea to automate their relationships with their customers entirely.

13

AUTOMATING SALES AND USER RELATIONSHIPS

Like all companies, Google has a sales department. Omid Kordestani, Google's head of Global Sales and Business Development, was among Google's first 40 employees. He has negotiated large contracts with AOL, Wal-Mart Stores, Inc., and other major companies. But the vast majority of sales at Google are automated—without any salespeople involved.

I say *automated* where others might use the term *virtualized*. The term I'm using, which better describes the process, alludes to industrial concepts of productivity and efficiency as well as fears about putting people out of work. Companies in other sectors have since adopted this major innovation in their own businesses. To name only two travel companies, Easyjet and idTGV (the online sales outlet of the French national railway) have instituted automated sales systems similar to Google's.

For many years, programmers have attempted to automate parts of the sales process with Customer Relationship Management (CRM) or Sales Force Automation (SFA) software. Both types of programs attempt to automate the administration of customer relations, with varying degrees of success.

Google's system is radically different from either CRM or SFA: It totally automates the sales transaction *and* fulfills the order. The typical Google advertiser has no contact with a live person. No salesperson contacts him or her, tries to persuade him or her of anything, or negotiates prices. Everything happens between the buyer and the computer—or rather between the buyer and the Google application.

In Chapter 2, I discussed how Google's automated sales model greatly reduces transaction costs and enables it to reach advertisers far too small for other media. In this chapter, I'll discuss the impact of this advance on organization and management.

Eliminating Conflicts Between Sales and Marketing Departments

Every company experiences conflicts between its sales force and its marketing department. Salespeople are expected to contact customers, present products, negotiate prices, and close sales. That is their real work. But they are also expected to generate reports, maintain customer records, and fill out forms. This information, in turn, is used by the operations and marketing departments to define production schedules, formulate marketing strategies, and launch advertising campaigns.

Unfortunately, the salesperson's dual responsibilities are in conflict because they involve entirely different skills. Salespeople everywhere complain, at least to some extent, about all the "red tape" and paperwork. In fact, in some companies, red tape consumes as much as 50 percent of a salesperson's time. Sales managers sometimes get fixated on making sales quotas, and they chastise those who don't meet monthly goals, so the paperwork often falls behind. Conversely, a salesperson who devotes the requisite time to completing administrative chores may be criticized for falling behind in making sales calls.

This contradiction explains the chronic weakness found in many sales departments, the dissatisfaction they generate at most companies,[*] and marketing staffers' frustration with the poor quality of information received.

By fully automating the sales process, Google eliminates these conflicts. Information comes directly from the customer and is sent directly to the people who need it most—including the marketing department—as well as upper management, engineers, and product planners.

NOTE   *In Chapter 9 I mentioned that Eric Schmidt received information every two hours about the spreadsheet that Google had just launched. In a traditional company, he would have waited weeks for a formal report from the marketing department. In how many companies would the CEO spend even a second looking at this type of information?*

Automation also eliminates another fundamental source of tension between the sales and marketing departments: conflicts over prices and featured products. Management wants to market products with high margins, but salespeople want to sell products that are easy to move and that raise their commissions. With Google's automated auction, conflicts over pricing disappear as the price is set by the consumer without Google's interference.

The arguments over new products, an indirect obstacle to innovation in most companies, also vanish. Before marketing a new product, a company has to "sell" it internally to the salespeople, who need to be motivated to devote time to the new product without neglecting older products. They need training, new product literature, and new sales tools to present to customers. To prevent errors in marketing

---

* According to an Accenture study in 2004, 56 percent of leaders in large companies rated the performance of their sales forces as "average, mediocre, or catastrophic." According to a more recent study, executives gave their sales managers a score of 7 out of 10 possible points. Tom Atkinson and Ron Koprowski, "Finding the Weak Links," *Harvard Business Review* (July–August 2006).

information and to avoid alienating the sales force who often approach new products with a healthy dose of skepticism, marketing people typically spend a considerable amount of time on research and preparation before presenting new products to the sales force.

But all of this preparation takes time and money and delays the launch of new products.

Complete sales automation eliminates this obstacle to growth as well: the time needed to build and train a sales staff. Studies show that companies with strong growth need to anticipate and recruit salespeople before the companies grow if they don't want to miss out on sales early in a product's lifecycle. Companies have to invest in new salespeople *before* launching a major new product; making that commitment requires not only confidence in the company's future growth but also the resources to finance and equip these people. If companies train salespeople for a product that fails, they risk overextending their finances and taking significant losses. But, at the same time, if they don't expand their sales force prior to product release and wait instead until the last moment, they're forced to do emergency recruiting, lower their selection criteria, and send out undertrained representatives.

Automation also changes the strategies of players and eradicates two well-known perverse effects. First, it renders useless the customer tactic to delay a purchase until the supplier has no option but to cut prices. In some industries, including software, many customers wait until the end of a quarter or a year to make purchases. They know that salespeople who need to make their quota will bargain so they can close out the quarter or the year with higher total sales. This delay unbalances the salesperson's workload and drives prices lower than the marketing department's projections.

Second, automation also reduces another perverse effect of commission sales, one that frequently victimizes companies specializing in new technologies. It goes like this: A salesperson delays or advances the date of a sales contract by a few days in order to maximize his or her income. If the salesperson has doubts about his or her future with the company (or, worse, doubts about the company's future), the salesperson will get his or her customers to close sooner in order to maximize sales that will determine the bonus for that period. Or, if the salesperson is confident in his or her future and that of the company, he or she might delay the contract a few days for tax reasons.

These shuffles artificially skew the results used by company managers to calculate sales forecasts. If these manipulations occur infrequently, they don't matter much, but if all the salespeople do the same thing at the same time, the forecasts will be off, leading to bad relations with investors who may think they have been deceived. (Several companies have been severely sanctioned by the financial markets for making artificially inflated forecasts based on bogus end-of-year sales figures reported by salespeople.)

In both cases, sales automation smoothes out cycles and enhances the accuracy of management information.

Understanding User Behaviors

By obtaining more direct information on what users do, a company can bring its customers closer to everyone involved in supplying the products. At the same time, engineers tend to abandon the defensive attitude they often display when marketing staff or salespeople try to give them advice on what products to create.

Odd as it may seem, customers have a singular advantage over all these professionals: They make the ultimate decision about a company's future products and services. And, ironically enough, sales automation actually improves the ability of those in charge of the company to listen to their customers. By "depersonalizing" the sales process, managers are able to follow and observe actual customer behavior, thereby receiving an infinitely richer information source than the usual demographic categories used by marketing people, such as occupation, income, and age.

Sales automation also eliminates the skewing that can affect surveys, opinion polls, and reports from salespeople. (Researchers who delve into these issues—including sociologists, ethnologists, and marketing experts—stress that the observation of actual behaviors generally produces very different results from those derived from polls based on statements.[*])

---

[*] In the field of marketing, a whole body of literature is devoted to observation of customer behaviors. The articles conclude that this research method is highly efficient in the quality of information it provides but very costly. Of course, automating the customer relationship decreases the cost.

Finally, sales automation eliminates the potential mismeasurements caused by self-consciousness and rationalization. Automation improves the accuracy of behavior measurement because users can't adjust their answers to suit their own standards of acceptability or what they think is expected. For example, a study done at Ball State University using real-world measurements suggests that people actually use the Internet twice as much as they say they do on questionnaires.[1]

But Where Did My Sales Rep Go?

Sales automation clearly has many advantages, but it can't completely eliminate all shortcomings, mistakes, and difficulties. At Google, as with any service company, some incidents require human intervention.

Although search engine users rarely complain about the quality of service they receive, those who maintain forums and blogs and the advertisers that work with these sites do. Bloggers complain about not seeing their site in search results. Did my site disappear because of a decision made by Google or because of a flaw in the algorithm? Advertisers complain about incorrect charges. "As a representative of companies that spent more than $300,000 on your AdWords program, I am writing this letter to you in the hope that someone will respond to me," wrote one customer who was unhappy with the lack of response from a salesperson assigned to him. "Why," he went on, "does Google treat me badly like a vagrant trying to buy a cup of coffee for a dime at McDonald's?"[2]

This leads to a final point about the downside of automation (for corporations)—that is, the emergence of greater consumer power (an upside, of course, for the consumer).

When things go wrong in a traditional business, the problem is nearly always handled privately—whether by phone, email, snail mail, or a meeting. In the new virtual marketplace, without personal contact, correspondence, or meetings, a dissatisfied customer may turn to the Internet, post a message on a blog or forum, and thereby inform a large group of customers about his or her problems. Complaints thereby pass from the private sphere to the public domain, which creates a new problem for the company.

This public method of complaining is often the only way to reach a company with a complaint and can exert far stronger pressure than a private complaint. Many companies seldom pay much attention to dissatisfied customers, but they are far more attentive to those who display their discontent publicly because these complaints can have far-reaching effects on the company's reputation.

14

PUTTING USERS IN CHARGE

Once consumers were kings. Now they've become tyrants.[1]

—McKinsey & Company

Some companies have risen to fame surrounded by armies of enthusiasts (like Apple), while many others—like big oil, chemical companies, armament manufacturers, and agribusiness—have faced hostile press campaigns. But never before has a company like Google been constantly under the eyes of millions of observers throughout the world.

Online Communities: A New Force

Scores of blogs are devoted to news about Google, its projects, and its products. Some, like Google Blogoscoped (*http://blogoscoped .com/*) by Philipp Lenssen, focus on monitoring the company. Still others, like Ogle Earth (*http://ogleearth.com/*) deal only with specific tools like Google Earth, the company's mapping service.

Estimating the total volume of these ongoing communications about Google in the blogosphere isn't easy, but by all indications, the numbers are probably huge. According to Technorati, a company that specializes in observing the blogosphere, many thousands of comments tagged with the word *Google* are posted daily on blogs. For example, as you can see in a recent 180-day snapshot of blog posts tagged *Google* (see the figure below), an average day brings somewhere in the range of 4,000 to 6,000 posts. Compare this activity with tags like *Obama*, *life*, *Apple*, and even simply the word *search*, and the tag *Google* is a clear standout.

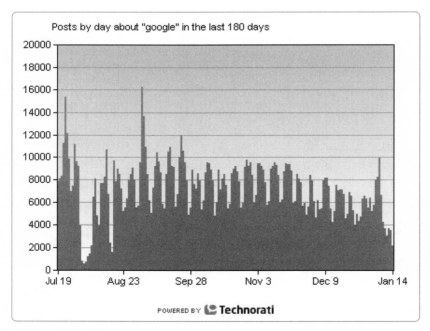

Google on Technorati, July 2008 through January 2009

Whatever we take this data to mean, it seems clear that Google is talked about quite a lot (though one can't weed out the simple use of the term *google* to mean *search*, since the word has entered the vernacular). When we recognize that these blog comments are, in turn, read by tens of thousands of Internet surfers who also talk among themselves in forums and newsgroups, we can see how broad the discussion is likely to be.

Bloggers who regularly comment on Google come from diverse fields. They include journalists like John Battelle, users fascinated by technology, ad customers, people selling site-design and optimization services, and current and former Google employees. They even include human rights advocates, like the creators of a blog that denounces censorship in the People's Republic of China (*http://savegooglefreechina .org/*); people concerned about protection of individual liberties; and many more. Their audience is also varied, including subscribers who receive message feeds regularly and "passersby" who visit only occasionally.

Authors, subscribers, and casual readers constantly move about, circulating among groups. Like bees carrying pollen from flower to flower, they distribute information. Every time something about Google is mentioned, some of those who heard about the news will share that tidbit with other groups, link to the information, and share their comments and critiques. Thus the news circulates within each zone of influence.

This process of diffusing information is fast and highly effective. In a few hours, the whole community knows the latest. For example, those who first learned of Google's acquisition of Writely, an Internet-based word processor, spread the news to tens of thousands without any help from Google.

These new modes of information dissemination build media bridges between topics that might otherwise remain separate. This cross-pollination creates relationships among individuals who live in different intellectual universes, allowing them to share lucky finds, viewpoints, and breaking news. Far from the customary image of the solitary Internet user in front of his or her computer screen, the

Internet continually weaves social bonds and produces what could be termed a *computer-assisted collective intelligence.*[*]

Online communities know no borders. Germans, Swedes, Norwegians, and the French are no less active than Americans per capita. The efforts of non-Americans, however, tend to be more successful if they blog in English. Political frontiers may have disappeared on the Web, but linguistic barriers remain, even though only 30 percent of blogs are written in English.[†] This creates an unusual geography of information, with dark zones and *terra incognita*. When Brazilian authorities demanded information from Google about web surfers who used its Orkut community site for illicit activities, the blogosphere remained strangely silent, even though earlier similar requests from the US government had caused an uproar. One might assume, of course, that few members of the community at large can read Portuguese.

Communities Serving the Company

Leveraging the power of online communities as a marketing resource is nothing new, and many technology companies have been doing this for years. But Google was the first to recognize the full importance of these virtual communities and to analyze the many ways it could employ them to further its own growth.

Like Microsoft, Apple, and others, Google gives away application programming interfaces (APIs) that help users develop mini-applications to complement Google tools. Most of these mini-applications are just gadgets used to personalize the home page, the toolbar, or the desktop. But developers can use these APIs to extend Google gadgets, like Google Maps, building *mashups* that combine data from different sources to create new applications that solve real problems, and bring traffic to Google.

---

* This collective intelligence has assumed many varied forms: When customers shop for a book, Amazon.com provides them with a list of books bought by other readers. This listing may offer customers more clarity than many actual comments about the book. Alexa does the same with websites and their visitors. Delicious, Kaboodl, and Furl allow users to build libraries or public collections of pages, providing more alternatives to pool individual research efforts similar to those found in *wikis*, the tool used to create Wikipedia articles.

† According to David Sifry of Technorati, which publishes periodic surveys of the blogosphere.

SketchUp is another good example of how Google has been able to leverage the efforts of volunteers. This 3D modeling tool (acquired when Google purchased @LastSoftware, a small startup) was released in a free version with the sole aim of enabling users to build applications that would extend Google Earth in interesting ways.

Google has extended this cooperative volunteer effort into areas that most companies would retain for themselves, such as translating pages, new product introductions, and indexing images (for image search). In fact, Google is available in 130 languages today only because volunteer hobbyists get together regularly to exchange tips and tricks about the best way to translate documentation. And when Google introduces images searchable by category, with captions, it will be able to do so because of these contributions. (The company even invented a game called Image Labeler, wherein a participant scores points—with no tangible value—each time his or her entry matches those of other players who propose captions for images displayed by the software.)

But why would people volunteer to work for free for a company as profitable as Google? Their motivations are diverse. Some jump in just to be part of a Google project and to compete with other skillful programmers. Others contribute out of philanthropy or in the interests of activism: Volunteer translators want to see their language gain greater currency on the Internet. "It's enough to see my mother using the Danish version of Google," said one volunteer translator. The quality of these volunteer translations is largely overseen by the volunteers: Users correct one another.

In all cases, these volunteers assemble around Google because of the tools provided and because they can prove their skills and demonstrate their achievements to the whole wide world.

These communities of volunteers have played a defining role in Google's rapid success. In fact, saying they are the reason for Google's success would not be an exaggeration. Without them, Google probably wouldn't be the market leader that it is today. The volunteers offer not only pools of expertise in which Google can fish for assistance but also a rich source of market research. The minute a new idea emerges, community members are on top of it, discussing it and speculating on its chance of success. Where conventional companies must resort to traditional market research to discover what their users want, Google has only to listen for the rustle of ideas in the conversations of its followers. The trends that interest marketing professionals are evident in their beginning stages as users examine, analyze, and recommend changes to new products. And, not surprisingly, these conversations also play a determining role in publicizing new products.

The Rogers Diffusion Model

The technology adoption lifecycle is often illustrated by the normal bell curve popularized by Everett Rogers in his book *Diffusion of Innovations*, published in 1962. In his work, Rogers segments purchasers into five categories: innovators, early adopters, early majority, late majority, and laggards, as shown here.[2]

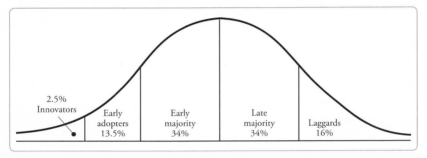

The five categories of technology adopters

The rate of product adoption and purchase behavior is related to psychological and sociological factors. Innovators actively seek information about new ideas, with a focus on novelty. Early adopters, on the other hand, consider the benefits that an idea or product affords. The early majority deliberates for some time before adopting a new idea, whereas the late majority approaches innovation with a "skeptical and curious air" and does not adopt it until most others have done so. Early adopters are opinion leaders—the people others go to for their view on new products.

The Bass Diffusion Model

The Rogers model is easy to understand and apply to new product releases, but unfortunately, it has become a bit old fashioned. Most marketing theorists now prefer the Bass diffusion model pioneered in 1969 by Frank Bass, an academic who is often referred to as a founder of scientific marketing.[3]

The Bass diffusion model (shown here) describes the process of product adoption as the result of the interactions between users and potential users. The Bass model hinges on the interplay of three factors: market size, innovation (customers who buy without being influenced by the current state of the market), and imitation (customers whose buying decisions are influenced by others).

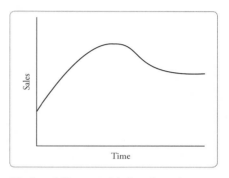

The Bass diffusion model of product adoption

In the Bass model, the coefficients of innovation and imitation are not fixed, as in Rogers's theories, but variable. In other words, purchase behaviors are not related to psychological factors. No particular set of people is thought to be more naturally prone to being pioneers than imitators (a fact that has been confirmed by research). The person who buys a PC as soon as it is introduced may delay buying that hot new mobile phone and may not own a digital camera. People do not fall into discrete and fixed categories.

Bass also offers an explanation of imitation: "Imitators 'learn,' in some sense, from those who already bought."[4] Thus, he introduces into his analysis the concepts of competence (you don't ask the same person for advice about both choosing a dress and choosing a car) and learning time, which is never instantaneous.

In the Bass model, the coefficient of *innovation* depends on the number of innovators (those who talk about their technical choices and act as opinion leaders) and the depth of their social networks. The coefficient of *imitation* depends on the frequency of contacts between prospective customers and these opinion leaders. The more innovators a prospective buyer meets, the more influential their cumulative opinion becomes. What the first person said is reinforced by the second and so on.

The growth of online communities hasn't really changed the Bass model; they've simply put it on steroids and yanked the Bass curve toward the top left of the graph by doing the following:

- Broadening the market so it is no longer limited to demographic segments defined by marketing objectives or to sales outlets defined by distribution channels.

- Increasing public exchanges among innovators and turning ordinary people into opinion leaders.

- Multiplying points of view and opinion, thereby reducing the learning time needed by imitators and accelerating the rate of adoption.

- Widening social networks, thereby increasing the leaders' zones of influence. A blogger who has just tested a product in California can almost instantly reach one or even thousands of imitators in Finland or Australia.

Finally, online communities have multiplied the contacts between imitators and innovators. All it takes is a bit of curiosity on the part of a potential imitator to quickly find opinion leaders who are ready to answer his or her questions (or search for already archived answers).

Enhancements to the Product Adoption Models

Over the years, the Bass model has been enhanced by the addition of other potential mechanisms that help explain Google's dominance.

Some authors have replaced the concept of learning time with conformism. Their assumption is that consumers, who are not experts and who lack the time or desire to obtain expert information, are happy to trust the majority vote and choose the most successful products. This argument, recently advanced by D.E. Smallwood and J. Conlisk, helps explain why the best products don't always win.[5] In Google's case, this argument explains why new users simply flock to its search engine: They don't take the time to ask experts; they just follow the leaders.

Other theorists, like Albert Bemmaor, a marketing professor at the ESSEC management school in France, have added a psychological element to the Rogers Diffusion Model in an attempt to improve its predictive accuracy. Bemmaor and others speak of a measurable propensity to buy, which may be higher in some than in others. They explain that initial purchasers of a new and largely unknown product take higher risks than those who follow. As a consequence, only those who aren't intimidated by the risk will make the leap. In order to reduce this risk, these pioneers share information that they uncover in the media and in newsgroups. By supporting these exchanges, communities help to reduce risk with discussions that allow people to narrow their options and generally accelerate the rise to power of products, standards, and suppliers deemed to be the best and most reliable.

Communities and Word of Mouth

The increasing influence of online communities has spurred renewed interest among marketing specialists in understanding the way that information travels by word of mouth. Many companies have been created to leverage relationships with online communities, often called *social media marketing*, but this metaphor must be viewed with caution. Despite some similarities between communities and word of mouth, the phenomena are different.

Traditional word of mouth typically affects only a relatively close circle of people at first. Information travels within small groups who share similar interests. If you were to draw a chart of the spread of ideas by word of mouth, the chart would look like leopard spots. In contrast, because the boundaries of online communities are not limited by proximity, information can travel much more widely. Online communities lend themselves to the support and growth of dominant products and comprehensive standards. They are also more likely to be selective: The exchanges and rapid discussion among pioneers support the adoption of the best solutions and inhibit the development of low-quality products, which may not be the case with word-of-mouth dissemination.

Watching Every Minute

The communities that have been built around Google form a kind of monitoring system that evokes Jeremy Bentham's *Panopticon*, a type of all-seeing prison in which no action can be hidden. As with open source software development, every time a new function or tool goes live online, the community responds with questions about the product and what it's good for. Users test the tool and share their analysis and experience. The often ruthless tests they devise are thoroughly and frequently discussed.

Strategy is also monitored closely by these communities; none of Google's decisions escapes dissection, analysis, and discussion. Questions like these are asked: Why this initiative? Why now? What does Google expect to gain? Is Google's release of the Chrome web browser a frontal attack on the dominance of Microsoft's Internet Explorer, or is it just another tool to deliver Google apps?

Ultimately, this oversight boils down to ethical questions. Whatever their origin, members of the blogosphere have a common conviction: Search engines, blogs, and other Internet tools will revolutionize the world and the way we live by bringing people together in expanded virtual communities. Thus, concern about the moral or policy implications of any web tool, as well as its performance, is legitimate.

Four topics come up regularly in these discussions:

Protection of private data   How far can search engines go?

Censorship   Does Google have the right to censor information?

Dishonest use of technology   How can phishing and click fraud be stopped?

Intellectual property rights   Who can make "fair use" of what?

As you can see here, conversations about these ethical issues follow a specific pattern: If peaks occur sometimes, as with censure (at the time of this survey, Google was under strong criticism for having made an agreement with Chinese authorities allowing them to block certain sites), the "noise" is usually continuous. The blogosphere rarely interrupts its surveillance.

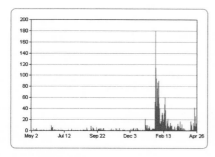

Censorship in China

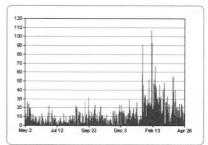

Protection of private data

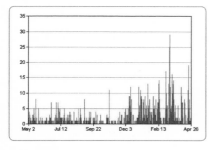

Click fraud

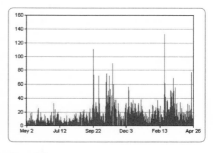

Copyright

Number of mentions, according to Technorati

Ethical questions play a key role in the Internet industry because the industry is largely unregulated and a moving target: Legislation can hardly keep up with it. Nobody knows when new legislation will be enacted to enforce regulations that govern copyright, royalties, and protection of privacy, let alone what the laws will cover or how they will be enforced. Internet users are all the more attentive to Google's behavior because they're well aware that currently only a voluntary code of ethics (perhaps one akin to Hippocrates' famous "Do no harm") can prevent the company from behaving badly.

A Genuine Influence

Naturally, Google management can't afford to ignore what online communities say, and it doesn't. Each day, managers and engineers receive detailed summaries of comments about the company and its products. The smallest defect is immediately spotted, noted, and broadcast—not only to the company's own employees but also to the general public via the media. Many influential publications like *The Economist* feature blog comments and analyses drawn from online discussions about Google.

Because of the strength and influence of these online communities, Google's only choice once a problem is identified is to fix it fast, which became clear when Google had to revamp the first version of its video search engine, Google Video, because of user complaints.

These communities also prod Google into action: Any lag behind the competition generates immediate comments and criticism. Were Google to stop improving its products for a few weeks or a few months, widespread speculation about possible problems, challenges, and "creative breakdowns" would ensue. And because financial analysts and journalists follow these blogs, the company's image would soon suffer, followed closely by its stock price.

Repeated questions about Google's strategy finally convinced the company's leaders to state their objectives more clearly—which they did in mathematical terms, of course. This trend began at a conference of financial analysts in early 2005, and since then a number of interviews have been published, including one with Marissa Mayer that appeared in *Der Spiegel* in April 2006. In her interview Mayer explained the 70/20/10 approach, which Google uses to allocate time between its core business and its other products. Seventy percent of all effort goes into search and advertising, 20 percent into satellite products (like Gmail, Google Print, and Google Earth), and 10 percent is reserved for less grand ideas like Orkut. Mayer's answer was skillful in that it at once satisfied both the financial community by reassuring them that most effort is devoted to the company's core business and the blogosphere by addressing their main concern, which is innovation.[6]

The agreement that Google struck with Chinese authorities shows how seriously Page and Brin take community opinion. Like many executives in similar circumstances, they could have issued a vague press release in response to this crisis and waited for the storm to blow over. They could have waited to respond until the major news media and congressional committees had fully addressed the issue. Instead, they first responded to the surrounding communities in their own language with a message on the official Google blog.

Rather than make justifications or excuses, they described their concern, their equivocation, and the debate that had taken place among those at the top of the company who wanted to proceed at any cost and those who were concerned about the moral and political issues:

> Launching a Google domain that restricts information in any way isn't a step we took lightly. For several years, we've debated whether entering the Chinese market at this point in history could be consistent with our mission and values. Our executives have spent a lot of time in recent months talking with many people, ranging from those who applaud the Chinese government for its embrace of a market economy . . . to those who disagree with many of the Chinese government's policies, but who wish the best for China and its people. We ultimately reached our decision by asking ourselves which course would most effectively further Google's mission to organize the world's information and make it universally useful and accessible. Or, put simply: how can we provide the greatest access to information to the greatest number of people?[7]

This utilitarian rationale, straight out of Jeremy Bentham (the net sum of pains and pleasures), continues the author of the blog, led to this decision:

> Filtering our search results clearly compromises our mission. Failing to offer Google search at all to a fifth of the world's population, however, does so far more severely.

In later comments, Page even suggested that Google's entry into the People's Republic of China had the positive effect of raising awareness of censorship.[8] This observation wasn't entirely false, judging both by the volume of questions posed on the topic in English as well as in Chinese and as revealed by analyses of questions about Google. Still, economic considerations were never raised—as if they were unimportant.

Reputation as a Motivating Force

Online communities not only influence Google, they also serve as guardians of one of the company's major assets: its reputation.

Everyone would agree that a company's reputation is important, but just how important was precisely measured only when eCommerce prompted economists and marketing analysts to take a closer look. In their study titled, "The Value of Reputation on eBay: A Controlled Experiment,"[9] these researchers tracked the sales of postcards, electric guitars, comics, and even Gmail invitations (when Google distributed its mail application by invitation only) on eBay. They then expanded their research to compare the performance of well-known sellers and newcomers. Their conclusions? A good reputation helps not only to sell things but also at higher prices. The variations are significant, with 5 percent more total sales at prices averaging more than 6 percent higher when Gmail invitations were used.

A good reputation also changes perceptions. For example, studies carried out using a blind-taste-test principle give Google an unquestionable advantage. Specifically, when a page of search results was shown to 1,000 Internet users, it satisfied 800 of them when the page was labeled as Google results. On the other hand, when the same users were shown an unlabeled screen of the same results, slightly more than 700 were satisfied.[*]

All of this suggests that once you've established a good reputation, preserving it is worthwhile. You'll also need to deserve that reputation, however. And you'll need to build awareness and prevent any confusion by consistently imprinting your trademark image in the minds of consumers—right? That's what most communication specialists believe, but they're wrong.

Doug Edwards, the graphic artist who was in charge of the Google home page in the late 1990s, described his surprise and concern when Sergey Brin wanted to make changes to the Google logo:

> One of the few convictions I brought with me to Google, based on the two books I had read about branding, was that

---

[*] Similar results were reported by Jansen, Zhang, and Zhang in "The effect of brand awareness on the evaluation of search engine results," CHI, 2007, *http://portal.acm.org/citation.cfm?id=1241026*.

you needed to present your company's graphic signature in a maniacally consistent manner; to pound it into the public consciousness with a thousand tiny taps, each one exactly the same as the one before. . . .

So I was caught by surprise when Sergey suggested that he wanted to play with our logo on the home page. Remember, this was not only the most prominent placement of our signature logo, it was the only placement of our signature logo. We weren't advertising on TV or on billboards or in print. The logo floating in all that white space was it. And we were hardly so well known in 1999 that we could assume people already had our brandmark burned into their brains.[10]

Brin got his way, and as Edwards recognizes today, Brin was right: The quality of Google's algorithm, its products, and its services is what built the company's reputation—not its logo.

The New Stakeholders

For moralists, actively seeking a good reputation presents an ethical quandary. Spinoza, a 17th-century philosopher, wrote, "Fame has the further drawback that it compels its votaries to order their lives according to the opinions of their fellow-men, shunning what they usually shun, and seeking what they usually seek."[10] For the purposes of this book, this statement means that in order to maintain a good reputation, individuals and companies need to agree with their market and their customers.

For companies like Google, which operate in a market where a good reputation is a major asset, complying as closely as possible with the interests of its customers offers a powerful incentive. Communities act as *stakeholders* in the company's governance. Stakeholders are, according to R. Edward Freeman who originated the concept, "people or groups who can affect or who are affected by a company."[12]

These communities of stakeholders don't have representatives on Google's board of directors, as do shareholders and employees, but by giving a voice to consumers who usually lack one, they move the boundaries and shift the balance of power. By performing some functions that are normally the tasks of sales or marketing departments at other companies, online communities have reinforced engineering skills at the expense of management and technostructure, and they counterbalance the influence of those who would change the company's economic model. (Articles about Google in the financial press emphasize that having only one source of income—advertising—is risky business.[13] Whether this is true doesn't matter; the stock market believes it's risky, so its constituents continue to pressure Google to stop providing services for free.)

But of all the battles taking shape, the most important will concern personal data, the outcome of which will determine the growth of Google and all search engines. In this case, the opposing sides are distinct and the balance of power is complex, but you can be sure the online communities will be there. Overall, Google can expect to find within its communities some expert partners who share both its desire for technological development and its sensitivity to the fears of its more faint-hearted users.

Lauren Weinstein is one expert who straddles both worlds. A data processing developer, he collaborated on the initial development of ARPANet, the military forerunner of the Internet. As an ardent defender of privacy rights, he has sometimes been highly critical of Google through his blog at *http://lauren.vortex.com/*. But when Google management asked him to explain his point of view, he addressed the engineers. His question to them was, could they come up with a solution?

In an open letter to the company, Weinstein asked Google to create a team dedicated to the protection of individual users, with the goal of ensuring that Google products meet numerous acceptable standards. In response, some months later, Google nominated a privacy counsel.

On this issue, as with many others, users have imposed their own rules. Because of their strong impact on its reputation, it is easy to conclude that Google's users have become a kind of partner with Google, and their opinions are nearly impossible to ignore.

In general, the concept of "stakeholders" is associated with ownership—parties who control part of a company's assets, whether capital for shareholders or skills and expertise for employees. Online communities give consumers the capacity to affect another significant company asset: Its reputation and the value of its brand. This is what *BusinessWeek* called "brand democratization,"[14] an expression that seems destined to endure. Through word of mouth and online communities, consumers are doing the true marketing of brands. Companies no longer own their brands; consumers do, and that's the power of putting users in charge.

PART IV
Challenges and Risks

Quarter after quarter, reading each Google financial report has been like watching the birth of a giant. As always, people tend to speculate about what might slow the company's progress and cripple its growth. Does the Colossus have feet of clay? Where might difficulties arise?

This exercise helps identify the potential limits of the Google way. In the following chapters, I discuss the various ways in which Google's market has influenced the company's business and growth pattern. This discussion will, I hope, shed light on a very central question: To what extent can Google's contrarian strategies be emulated and adapted by managers at other companies?

Finally, I'll discuss the question of how well Google's model will be able to resist recessions and financial crises, like the one the world is experiencing as this book goes to press.

15

IS GOOGLE'S GROWTH SUSTAINABLE?

When Page and Brin recruited Eric Schmidt, they gave him a simple mandate: "Guide this fast-growing dotcom company into adulthood." Since then, Google has grown into a world leader in advertising, without compromising its core business of Internet search.

In 1998, email was the main web-based application, with search engines running far behind. In less than 10 years, and largely because of Google, the search engine has become indispensable throughout the world.

The Growth of Search

The numbers speak for themselves. For example, according to the Pew Internet & American Life Project, as of 2008, nearly half of all Americans use a search engine on a typical day, and the growth of that use is dramatic:

> The percentage of internet users who use search engines on a typical day has been steadily rising from about one-third of all users in 2002, to a new high of just under one half (49%). . . . Underscoring the dramatic increase over time, the percentage of internet users who search on a typical day grew 69% from January 2002, when the Pew Internet & American Life Project first tracked this activity, to May 2008, when the current data were collected. During the same six-year time period, the use of email on a typical day rose from 52% to 60%, for a growth rate of just 15%. These new figures propel search further out of the pack, well ahead of other popular internet activities, such as checking the news, which 39% of internet users do on a typical day, or checking the weather, which 30% do on a typical day.[1]

And the numbers continue to grow.

Search engines were originally conceived of as research tools, designed to be used to find that figurative needle buried in the Internet haystack. Today, search has become the main entry point to the Web and is used to find everything—specific websites, the age of a celebrity, the shortest route to a friend's house, the weather, scholarly research, and so on.

I would argue that this evolution only became possible because Google found a way to derive ad revenue from search without making the advertising intrusive and because the quality of Google's search results (*hits*) have continued to improve. But is this growth sustainable? Will Google's organizational structure allow the company to continue expanding at the current rate, as new markets, new competitors, and new problems and challenges emerge?

Google has tremendous assets and powerful resources to fight most of the battles to come, but as you shall see, these battles will have to be fought on several fronts including technical, legal, and economic. And the fight won't always be easy.

The Online Advertising Market

Let's begin our analysis with the main area in which Google competes: online advertising. As of this writing, the prognosticators in the economic press—*The Financial Times*, *The Economist*, and *The Wall Street Journal*, among others—have announced that the Internet advertising market is nearly mature. Their critiques, based on surveys by marketing professionals, forecast the end of two-digit growth. The response rates of advertising have, they say, become seasonal. As evidence, they cite a peak in the cost of clicks at the end of the year—for example, from US$26 in August 2005 to US$56 in December 2005. This seasonal shift comes as no surprise because sales typically rise during the fourth quarter of the year when people are out holiday shopping. According to these critics, the shift is a sign of maturity. That click prices rise and fall in proportion to the cost of advertising in traditional media indicates a slowing market. To support their thesis, journalists cite the deceleration of growth in the number of searches in the United States, the oldest Internet market. Thus, they say, Google can continue to grow only by increasing its market share at the expense of its competitors.

These analyses are fairly easily to counter. For one, the market for online advertising extends well beyond the United States. If market penetration is very high in North America (73 percent), Europe (48 percent) and Asia (15 percent) are expanding markets. And almost every quarter brings new ways of delivering ads, whether on blogs or through email, video, or social media.

Critics also cite technical arguments. For one, search, Google's specialty, makes up only 5 percent of total Internet activity. And no less important, visitors don't stay very long on Google's home page: They find what they're looking for and off they go. That means many people who use the Internet see only a limited number of the ads appearing in Google's search results, whereas ads are much harder to escape when they're delivered in email, in magazines, on television, in movie theaters, or on the radio.

The economic press also points to the difficulty of qualifying site visitors. Unless visitors log into a Google account or iGoogle before running their search, when they land on a page advertising a product, advertisers know nothing about their financial status, buying preferences, or likely age group. Google is clearly trying to solve this problem by offering personalized search (which is great for tracking users), but will that offering suffice?

Another challenge Google faces is that customers lured by Internet advertising are far more fickle than those targeted by other modes of advertising: They are only a click away from looking for a better price, and the cost of switching from one seller to another is low.

The challenges of online advertising are all valid concerns, but Google's results suggest that these challenges are not likely to dramatically affect its growth in the near term. For one, the number of searches that result in advertising impressions has increased steadily over time, and Google continues to dominate in search. Also, Google can add to its revenue from search-supported ads by running ads in other Google properties, like Gmail, Maps, and YouTube.

A more serious problem for Google could well be the current global economic recession. When companies face difficult economic conditions, they often cut their advertising budget. Of course, the deeper the recession, the deeper the cuts are likely to be and, like other companies that depend on those advertising dollars, Google should suffer as a result. However, as of this writing, Google does not appear to have been greatly affected. When hard hit by a recession, consumers spend more time searching for the best deals—and they can best do that on their favorite search engine. The United Kingdom, one of the economies hardest hit by the recession, provides a good illustration of this change in consumer behavior: Total retail sales fell by 0.8 percent in December 2008 compared with a year earlier, whereas Internet retail sales increased by 19.6 percent.[2]

Does this means Google is recession proof? Not necessarily. Google will feel the pinch if its main advertisers decide to cut their advertising budgets, as some did in late 2007 and 2008, but the company will suffer less than most other media. In the long run, Google could even profit from this economic crisis as more consumers search and shop on the Web.

New Competitors with Different Economic Models

These arguments invite a closer look at the Internet advertising market. As anyone who follows search advertising knows, Google dominates not only because it dominates the search market but also (and this reason is too often neglected) because Google delivers. Advertisers spend more on Google than any other search engine because it offers them the best results—the best *click-through rate* (*CTR*), the best conversion rate, cost-per-click, cost per order, and so on.

But all of this can change. Dominating the search market does not automatically translate into dominating the advertising market, and competing search engines are always working to improve their performance. (And they have smart engineers, too.) Advertisers can also choose to spend their dollars in other ways, whether in newspapers or magazines, on community sites like MySpace and Facebook, and so on. All of these players compete with Google, and each presents a real challenge to Google's dominance of the online advertising market.

One argument often made to support the company's dominance is that Google excels at mining data about its visitors that it then uses to serve tightly targeted ads. But Google is not alone in doing this. Some newspapers and magazines require you to subscribe to their print edition in order to read their online articles, but most provide free online content in exchange for membership registration. When visitors register, they provide these companies with the demographic information that advertisers need, which, in turn, allows traditional media to offer their advertisers precisely targeted ad campaigns that associate context with consumer profiles.[*]

Community or social media sites like MySpace and Facebook offer advertisers tightly targeted placements because they have extensive

---

* A top-of-the-line hotel can benefit from placing its ads in the travel pages of a newspaper only when those pages are seen by readers with a high income. This can go a step further: A reader who regularly visits the travel pages probably travels a lot. Airlines, travel agencies, and hotel chains can present their offers as soon as that reader arrives at the home page of his or her favorite newspaper, even if he or she is there to read a news article or check out the business section. These noncontextual ads are often quite effective—people who frequent pages devoted to dieting or fashion are more likely to click a targeted ad when they're reading an article about something else. The ad topic interests them just as much, but the ad isn't competing with the article for their attention.

and precise information on their user's age, gender, location, and interests. Advertisers don't need to analyze profiles and contextual impressions with a social media tool—users do that work already.

Whether they target small or large advertisers (like traditional media) these players are favored by advertising professionals. Because they make their living by selling research studies and producing ads, these professionals use every opportunity to criticize the Google model. Laura Desmond, director of MediaVest, the buying service for Coca-Cola and Gillette, says that if Google and Yahoo! want to sell ads for mass-market products and continue to increase advertising sales, they will have to change their economic model. Why, these critics argue, should major brands follow Google's rules? Do they need to accept the minimalist ads that bypass the talents of their marketing departments and ad agencies? Why should they place ads in the blogosphere, where customers go to praise (or, more likely, criticize) their products?

Imagining the conversations between advertisers and their marketing consultants is easy. The first camp demands tests of these new media, whereas the second tries to dissuade the first camp with the blend of arrogance and aggressiveness sometimes seen within their ranks. The arguments become more heated as new agencies that specialize in behavioral marketing and Internet research compete with traditional ad agencies.

The debates become even more intense as managers of large brands worry about diluting their advertising budget. The Méridien hotel chain filed a lawsuit against Google for trademark infringement. Méridien argued that when Internet surfers used Google to search for Méridien, they were shown ads with links to the company's competitors. Companies around the world have continued this argument with varied results: Axa, Louis Vuitton, and Bourse des Vols, a travel agency, in France; Geico Insurance and the American Blind & Wallpaper Factory in the United States; and metaspinner media in Germany. Courts have also had to rule on companies' complaints that claimed a competitor had used their trademark to attract Internet surfers to the competitor's site by slipping the competitor's name into the HTML code to attract search engine hits.

For these plaintiffs the value of their brands is at stake, and the best-known brands are worth a lot. For example, according to the 2008 rankings by Interbrand, the value of the Coca-Cola brand is about $67 billion; Mercedes is worth $21 billion; and Apple and Louis Vuitton are worth about $6 billion each.[3] By allowing these brand names to be used, Google risks allowing formerly clandestine counterfeiters to publicize and enrich themselves at the expense of their large corporate victims by using click fraud and spam.

Click Fraud and Spam

Click fraud, the practice of clicking an ad hundreds or thousands of times to artificially increase the conversion rate, affects all advertisers and could, several experts say, become Google's Achilles' heel. Besides unscrupulous competitors, dissatisfied customers may use bogus clicks in an attempt to exact revenge, or site owners might generate fake clicks to boost their income from AdSense or a similar program that pays the owners every time an Internet surfer clicks ads displayed on the site.

According to companies specializing in auditing traffic quality, fake clicks cost Internet advertisers hundreds of millions of dollars and amount to about 15 percent of total clicks (advertisers surveyed by Outsell estimate that 14.6 percent of the clicks they're billed for are fraudulent; according to Click Forensics, the average overall industry click fraud rate was 16 percent for the third quarter of 2008).[4]

Google contests these figures, claiming they are greatly inflated.* The techniques used by these third-party auditors to gather data are, says Google, flawed. The auditors can't track the problem accurately because they don't have the necessary data. Figures are obtained by analyzing site visits, not by analyzing search engine data: Auditors don't have access to the *impression* data (how often an ad is viewed); they don't know the click-through rate for any given ad; and they ignore the percentage of clicks that Google has eliminated as "invalid." They often count as fraudulent return visits to a site and a return to a previous page or a reloaded page. In fact, as Alexander Tuzhilin,

---

* See, for instance, Andy Greenberg, "Counting Clicks," *Forbes.com* (September 14, 2007): *http://www.forbes.com/2007/09/13/google-shuman-fraud-tech-cx_ag_0914google.html.*

author of an in-depth study on the subject, explains, nobody, neither the search engines nor the advertisers, has the "comprehensive set of data pertinent to detect invalid clicks."[5]

Even if these figures are as exaggerated as Tuzhilin thinks and as Google claims (saying that no more than 0.02 percent of clicks are actually fraudulent), click fraud is a genuine threat that search engine companies don't take lightly—and it's a huge threat to the Internet economy. "Something has to be done about this really, really quickly, because I think, potentially, it threatens our business model," said George Reyes, then Google's chief financial officer, at a meeting with financial analysts in December 2004.[6] Other experts share his opinion.

Some observers, however, like George Jansen, an academic who studies these issues, argue that Google's payment system allows advertisers to compensate for click fraud. For example, if advertisers estimate that 15 percent of clicks are fraudulent, they can simply reduce their budget by that much. The scenario is an excessively optimistic one shared by Eric Schmidt, who said at a 2006 Stanford conference, "Eventually, the price that the advertiser is willing to pay for the conversion will decline, because the advertiser will realize that these are bad clicks; in other words, the value of the ad declines." He immediately added, however, "But because it is a bad thing, because we don't like it, because it does, at least for the short-term, create some problems before the advertiser sees it, we go ahead and try to detect it and eliminate it."[7]

Obviously, Schmidt's is the rational solution, especially because Yahoo! and Microsoft, when confronted with the problem, chose to address it and could use this as a competitive marketing ploy if Google fails to act. In fact, Google pays refunds to advertisers victimized by click fraud and has developed filters to subtract fraudulent clicks from customer invoices. But that is not enough and might even be counterproductive. After all, who knows if the filters work correctly or if Google really refunds every fraud victim?[*]

---

* Google could also give advertisers the option of prohibiting their ads from appearing on specific sites. Recently, it began to offer advertisements remunerated according to specific actions taken by Internet users, called *cost-per-action* (*CPA*). This is another way to fight fraud, although this method runs the risk of turning the advertisers into cheaters.

Click fraud is only one aspect of a more general phenomenon affecting the entire Internet: spam. The word *spam* was originally used in this context to describe unwanted mass email, but the term is now used to describe many types of phenomena; not all are fraudulent, but all attempt to subvert the system. "Spam is an arms race," says Douglas Merrill, an ex-Googler, adding that fooling search engines is a multimillion-dollar business.[8]

All spammers want to generate more hits and increase traffic to their pages. Some try to cheat the algorithm that ranks natural results in order to appear higher in search results. Others vie for a better position for their ad in the right column on the page.

Search engine spammers use several techniques to mislead search engines and their ad placement algorithms. The most common one is to build links between pages for reasons other than merit. These *nepotistic* links, as they are called, can be created by bombarding blogs and discussion forums with comments about a site and posting its link by soliciting outgoing links from other sites to decrease a competitor's ranking.* *Google bombing*, also called *link bombing*, describes attempts by spammers to raise the ranking of their page in Google's search results by increasing the number of pages that link to it, often by constructing *link farms*, dense networks of sites with reciprocal links. Another technique, called *cloaking*, is used to serve up a different page from those that the search engine "sees." For example, you search for information on "fertility among mosquitoes," and the search engine lists pages that, although they seem to the algorithm to answer your question, in fact, promote Viagra or Cialis.

The economic stakes are considerable. The success of these techniques is directly related to the behavior of Internet users, who typically read only the first page of results, if that much. Studies show that users visit the sites at the top of the first page of search results in 20 percent of searches and that they follow the ads at the top of the advertising column 10 percent of the time. More surprisingly, if

---

* This technique was used politically in 2004 to downgrade an anti-Semitic site that came in at first place on a search for the word *Jew*. Orchestrated by a journalist, the campaign asked Internet users to create outgoing links from their sites to the *Jew* page on Wikipedia. The campaign took one month (and 125,000 users) to achieve its desired goal. You can easily imagine how the same technique could be used in a hotly contested election campaign.

a site has both the top search position on the page *and* the top position in the ad column, users will click one or the other 60 percent of the time.* Needless to say, this phenomenon tempts spammers to mislead the classification algorithm.

These techniques are used by individual spammers as well as by consultants and individuals who offer their customers (including many large websites) a service designed to get their customers' sites listed on the first page of results by beating the algorithms behind PageRank. Unlike email spammers, their efforts to subvert search are particularly pernicious because they are almost invisible. People have learned how to recognize and protect themselves against email spam reasonably well, but manipulated search results are harder to recognize.

Search spam, which lowers the quality and reliability of search results, must be fought vigorously because it also deprives legitimate sites of the financial gains that derive from occupying a good PageRank position. And when some sites are successfully cheating, others are encouraged to cheat as well, which is a problem for everyone.

One response would be for Google to move its advertising model from cost-per-click to cost-per-action, wherein the advertiser would pay only when a visitor performs some predetermined action. That action might be reading a catalog, staying on the site for a certain length of time, providing personal information, or making a purchase. In fact, Google has adopted this scheme for large advertisers and now offers them advertising positions that are charged by volume.

Because the primary challenge is to detect web spam, however, the best solution will most likely be a technical one. Detection can be performed by analyzing links or page content, but this presents a difficult problem. In the absence of a definitive solution, search engines are condemned to adopt what military theorists call a *strategy of maneuver* in order to defeat their adversary, changing their algorithms regularly to disorient and confuse the enemy.

---

* All viewers see the topmost results, but only 10 percent of visitors see the bottom results (ranked 10). Fifty percent of visitors view the sponsored link at the top of the right column of the Google search page; the last ad, however, is seen by only 10 percent according to Enquiro and Didit, Eye Tracking Study, June 2005 (*http://www.enquiroresearch.com/eyetracking-report.aspx*).

But this tactic has its drawbacks: When a search engine changes its ranking algorithm, it risks hurting honest site owners. And because the algorithms are secret, this strategy can lead to suspicion that Google might not be honest in its ranking. These criticisms are the two most frequent ones leveled against the company.

Confidence and Privacy Concerns

Confidence and privacy concerns focus on the core of the company's business model. When advertisers criticize Google for not giving them accurate information about the people who click their ads, they bring up a touchy point. Google provides free search, and users do not have to register. So users haven't agreed to provide the information that advertisers want. But that doesn't mean Google lacks information about its customers. On the contrary, it knows a lot about them.

Google's customer information mostly derives from its collection of technical information through the use of *cookies* (small bits of code that are written to your hard drive by websites you visit) and *server logs*, which collect information using your machine's Internet address (IP number). Internet surfers are generally unaware that this information, which is of tremendous value, is being collected. Google can use the information to determine a visitor's geographical location, language, searches, and sites visited. Although this information contains nothing personal (age, sex, income, street address, or similar), it is actually pretty revealing.

As you search, search engines collect information about your behavior, and the more you search, the easier you are to profile. To get a sense of the power of this tracking information, imagine what law enforcement officers might infer from a list of the pages queried by a potential sex offender, terrorist, political activist, trade union member, or music pirate.

According to Kurt Opsahl, a Senior Staff Attorney with the Electronic Frontier Foundation (an organization that works to protect civil liberties on the Internet), Google and other search engines maintain "a massive database that reaches into the most intimate details of your life: what you search for, what you read, what worries you, what you enjoy. It's critical to protect the privacy of this information so people feel free to use modern tools to find information without the fear of Big Brother looking over their shoulder."[9]

Big Brother? Well, yes, but Google argues that it needs this information to give users high-quality results. Google will use a searcher's location (derived from his or her IP address) to tailor its results so that, for example, a person searching for a bank in the United Kingdom doesn't find one in Australia. Or, if a user's history shows that he or she visits sociology or philosophy sites, Google can tailor its results list to show sites of possible relevance to his or her most frequent searches. Knowledge of user preferences is the best way to reduce the imprecision that can slip into even the best-worded queries.

But—and this is a big but—keeping track of everything an individual says or does, including his or her opinions and decisions, is an erosion of that person's basic freedoms: the freedom to keep secrets and change opinions. A person is entitled to the anonymity that comes from personal data protection.

In response to these concerns, US authorities, persuaded by strident pleas from the direct marketing industry,* have chosen to focus on self-regulation to address this difficult issue. In comparison, European countries have passed legislation, beginning with the 1995 publication of a directive by the European Union giving its citizens statutory means to access their personal information, correct it, control it, and prevent its use for commercial purposes.

This difference is strongly underscored by philosophical issues concerning the role of the state and the objectives of personal data protection. In Europe, data protection is a question of individual dignity, whereas in the United States concern has focused on protecting public access to information.[10]

As you might imagine, self-regulation hasn't solved the problem, although ways to browse anonymously are available. In fact, experts rationalize why private data protection should disappear entirely in a digital world. "Technology and privacy are on collision courses.

---

* The Direct Marketing Association has successfully opposed many proposed regulations, beginning with an attempt to curb telemarketing in 1990—well before the development of the Internet as it's known today.

Technology makes [surveillance and tracking] cheap," said Sun founder Bill Joy at a public event. "The tip toward the public space being made less private . . . is one that's hard to fight."[11]

Whether they are jurists, economists, or specialists in new technologies, American professionals today are caught between the market and the legal system.[12] In essence, those who favor market sanctions and the right to control personal information are revisiting a problem discussed by Arthur R. Miller in his book *The Assault on Privacy*, which was published in 1971.[13] How, Miller asked, can we prevent the concept of personal data ownership from leading to the stifling of free expression? If I own information about myself, then I can stop others—especially journalists—from using it in the same way companies do when they legally attack consumers who criticize them too strongly. Jessica Litman, a professor at the University of Michigan Law School, adds, "One of the most facile and legalistic approaches to safeguarding privacy that has been offered to date is the notion that personal information is a species of property. If this premise is accepted, the natural corollary is that a data subject has the right to control information about himself and is eligible for the full range of legal protection that attaches to property ownership."[14]

Those who argue for judicial recourse think in terms of monetary damages. They want court actions restricted only to information whose misuse causes harm. But this opens the door to countless court cases like the one pursued by Ashley Cole, an Arsenal soccer player, who sued Google for linking his name to online news articles that implied he was bisexual.

This issue is critical for Google because it concerns the confidence placed in the company by its users, the loyalty of its advertising customers, and the development of some of its most promising markets.

Consider Internet applications for mobile phones. They present a major growth opportunity for Google because there are infinitely more mobile phones than computers, particularly in developing countries where almost everybody carries one. But mobile phone applications imply an increased confidence in the service provider because phones are used to access private data (diary, calendar, and notes, among others) stored on the service provider's servers. The same applies to services that allow marketers to collect personal data and track a user's whereabouts (based on searches for nearby restaurants, gas stations, pharmacies, and so on).

Healthcare information is another area that could impact Google's growth considerably. Each day, 7 percent of Internet users, or about 8 million American adults, search online for information about symptoms or a particular disease, to confirm a diagnosis, and so on.[15] Ensuring that the quality of the answers is definitive will require the development of a vertical solution similar to ones that Google has already developed to search academic resources (Google Scholar), patents (Google Patents), and programming code (Google Code), along with attendant utilities for reading the answers.

But again, the question of trust arises: The information that people search for when inquiring about their health reveals both their concerns and their personal health issues. Few, if any of us, would want our employers, the government, or a life or health insurance company to have access to this type of information unnecessarily. Will Google keep this information secure?

Google's long-term success will largely depend on how much trust its most demanding users place in it. This trust is all the more vital because Google's services are free; nothing prevents users from switching search engines and moving to a competitor.

Confidence is fragile and, as Google's leaders know, can quickly disappear if customers think their information is being exploited for the wrong reasons. To that end, in March of 2007, Google announced it would no longer store information indefinitely, stating "Unless we're legally required to retain log data for longer, we will anonymize our server logs after a limited period of time."[16] The blog post further stated, "We will continue to keep server logs dated (so that we can gradually improve Google's services and protect them from security and other misuse), but will make this data much more anonymous, so that it can no longer be identified with individual users, after 18–24 months."

Personal data protection is a sensitive matter in the United States and around the world, and breaches have ramifications. Yahoo! was sued for giving the Chinese police information on dissidents that led to their imprisonment.[17] But this question is also a sensitive one for governments themselves, who worry about important data stored

Can the Internet Reveal Classified CIA Information?

Experts at a British computer security company wondered how much information on the CIA, its programs, its installations, and its personnel was available in public databases.[18] Their fishing expedition was little short of miraculous. They could retrieve confidential phone numbers, secret site addresses, the site map of the internal network, domain names, servers, and the software programs on the CIA's computer system— ten pages of information that "The Company," as the agency is often called, would surely prefer to keep secret if only to avoid revealing its vulnerabilities to the whole world. Yet the information was all obtained legally, following British and US laws. You can only speculate about what information more devious, less law-abiding individuals might obtain from the records Google maintains about each of us.

in a foreign country. You don't have to be a conspiracy theorist to believe that the use of data collected by search engines can be sensitive; a simple query of public information databases already reveals quite a bit about organizations that are theoretically secretive—like the Central Intelligence Agency.

If governments decide to support the development of national search engines in Saudi Arabia, India, and Japan, as they have in Europe and the People's Republic of China, it won't be by accident. Governments are well aware that putting all the world's knowledge in the hands of an overseas company is, to put it mildly, imprudent. The United States is largely uninterested in regulating the Internet except for "good" reasons—to suppress pornography, pedophilia, and terrorism. But who knows whether that philosophy will change someday. Can Europeans, Japanese, or Chinese accept the notion that their researchers, strategists, and managers—all of whom use search engines regularly in their work—are at the mercy of a foreign power?

Google's dilemma is one of how to store the data it needs to improve the quality of its search results without betraying user trust. Its first solution is to purge regularly from its databases information that is no longer useful. The more vigorous defenders of privacy say this is not enough, however.

Another solution might be to have visitors opt in to allow Google to store their information, as it does with Web History. Web History allows you to find sites you've visited and build lists of bookmarks with just a mouse click, and when you sign up for the service, you give Google permission to track your web activity. The same is true of all Google applications, including your Google Account, Chrome (the Google browser), Google Docs, Gmail, iGoogle, and so on.

Will Copyright Concerns Slow Google's Growth?

Online delivery of film, video, and television are some of Google's most promising areas for growth and advertising sales. But like other companies interested in these emerging markets, Google has been confronted with a problem: copyright. Google can't simply take this content and deliver it without permission.

Finding a way around this obstacle, as Dailymotion, YouTube, and others did when they began hosting and streaming content produced by users, is possible. Coupled with the rise of cheap digital cameras and camcorders, these sites gave rise to an activity that might otherwise have remained marginal, at the same time opening a video market that few had suspected existed—one so large that within a few months, hundreds of thousands of videos were available online.

But this solution does not solve the problem of how to offer Internet access to copyrighted content. Hosting and search are two different activities. Whereas a search engine cannot be held liable for a document shown on its results pages (because it is only announcing the document's existence and providing a way to access it), hosting services are responsible for what they keep on their servers. This means that hosting services need to classify content, enforce rules, and refuse material that might invite lawsuits—whether that's pornography (which aficionados can find on specialized sites) or any material that might infringe copyrights, especially those belonging to big media conglomerates. The confusion between these two businesses can also lead a search engine to favor the content it hosts over content hosted elsewhere (as Google does when providing links to only the videos on its servers and those on YouTube—a policy that impacts the quality of results). A producer who wants the largest possible distribution will naturally be tempted to upload his or her video to multiple hosts, but this wastes his or her time and also degrades the results found on the few universal search engines.

But let's return to copyright and to the international laws that protect intellectual property—laws designed to give creators exclusive rights to their creations, protection against counterfeiters, and assurance of payment for their work, thereby providing an incentive to produce new artistic and commercial work. These laws were designed for and by an economy in which producing and distributing creative work was expensive. In that context, publishers, producers, booksellers, theater owners, broadcasters, and record distributors managed to control the major share of revenue from the sale and distribution of creative works—so they had a lot to lose with the arrival of digital technologies that limit the value or render useless many of their services. Today, almost anyone can publish a book or music online at almost no cost.

These mechanisms have to be reevaluated. The justification for protecting investments made by producers and editors makes less sense now that those costs have decreased. Why should Internet surfers pay the same price for a song, a book, or a film when the costs of production and distribution are virtually eliminated? A computer file is neither a disc nor a book. Paying for a recording medium or for the expenses of traditional distribution (including real estate or personnel) are no longer needed. The explosion of free amateur videos online has lessened the weight of the principal argument of copyright advocates—that artists wouldn't create new works without a system of copyright protection.

As long as these laws remain intact (and no indication exists that they will change quickly), Google will find it difficult to become the main gateway for the dissemination of copyrighted video and music. In 2007, only 39 percent of US Internet users employed a search engine to find videos.[19] By putting up obstacles to search-engine growth on video markets, copyright laws have given others an opportunity to enter this market.

Hulu, a joint venture of NBC Universal and News Corp, is a good example. Launched for public access in March 2008, eight months later Hulu had more than 206 million streams and 9 million viewers.[20] And Hulu could charge for all its videos when YouTube, the Google property, could only monetize 4 percent of its content.[21] The situation would change if copyright holders agreed to share advertising revenue, but that is only likely to happen if Google can guarantee them either higher revenues than they can expect from hosting the content on their own sites or significant additional revenues that won't cannibalize their own sales. In order to achieve revenue levels while offering visitors free access to content (paid for by advertising), Google will need to develop technology to index videos and insert contextual commercials that are more efficient than standard embedded TV commercials.[*] Until these technical innovations are underway, Google will have to make do with income from amateur videos, unless the company adopts a more classical economic model, like iTunes, where consumers pay for what they get.

Cultural Globalization and Resistance

In international markets Google might run into another obstacle: cultural resistance. Criticisms of Google and Yahoo! over censorship in the People's Republic of China were intense, and Google's leaders have since regretted their decision. From the beginning, Google has positioned itself as a totally international product, able to serve those who speak many different languages. Of course, saying they can't do it would be ridiculous, but how well can they really do this?

For each individual, language is part of his or her cultural capital, but American search engines don't treat languages equally. You hear all about the digital divide between those who are fully immersed in technology and those without access to it, but another, less obvious division exists between speakers of the languages search engines handle well and those they handle poorly. As you might guess, languages with non-English characters, such as Arabic, Chinese, Japanese, and Korean, present difficulties, and competitors have appeared in those countries.

Similar problems occur with languages that use the English alphabet such as French. Consider the two French words *loue* and *loué*. The first is a form of the verbs "to rent" and "to praise"; the second is at once the past tense of the same verbs and the name of a

---

[*] Several solutions are being considered, one of which consists of encouraging Internet surfers to add captions to their videos with tools provided by the host. The most sophisticated tools are based on analysis and transcriptions of the sound tracks of video files; analysis of the images themselves appears to be in the distant future.

region in Bresse famous for its poultry. As of this writing, the French version of Google doesn't differentiate between these two words, so entering either word will produce answers about renting an apartment, about praise, and about poultry. Slavic and Semitic languages have similar problems that lead to confusing and less useful results than you might expect.

Of course, these details will eventually be remedied, but they demonstrate a limitation of search engines in an environment in which English is spoken by only a portion of Internet users.

These weaknesses in the current global versions of the Google search engine have led to the development of competing regional products like Baidu, which has taken the lead in the Chinese market, and Yandex, which serves almost half of searches carried out in Russia, compared to Google's 33 percent share.[22]

Competing search engines may also be able to play on fears of cultural domination, which have emerged not only in Europe but also in Asia (especially China) and the Middle East. In 2006, France and Germany launched a European search engine called Quaero. Although it elicited many smirks in the United States, where it was immediately dubbed the "Google Killer," it has yet to be successful (in fact, as of this writing, it seems pretty dead), but its launch speaks to this concern about cultural hegemony. Around the same time and for the same reasons, Saudi Arabia announced its intent to cooperate with Germany in the development of Sawafi, an Arabic search engine. According to one expert, the initiative was made because "the number of home pages in Arabic accounts for only 0.2 percent of the total, while approximately 65 percent of Arab Net surfers do not read English and cannot read the English pages that represent more than 70 percent of the total."[23] The engine was never launched, but once again, the reasons behind this project did not disappear: Arabic culture is still not as prevalent as it should be on the Web.

Japan and India have also begun their own search initiatives. And in China, Baidu has long called itself the search engine that "knows Chinese best." Its TV commercials spoof a westerner with a big nose who thinks he knows everything but actually knows little if anything about the Chinese-speaking world. Baidu, a private company that benefits from official government support, has played the culture card and launched a "research center of cultural classics from before the Qin dynasty through the end of the Qin dynasty" in addition to an "open Chinese encyclopedia." As the *People's Daily* newspaper stated, "It is natural that the Internet was transformed into a cultural battlefield, and that cultural confrontations are felt more strongly there. In the era of the Internet, we need to defend our traditions, develop our technology, and confirm our presence."[24]

That says it all. American domination of the Internet amounts to a complete remapping of the cultural and intellectual landscape. Not only is English the dominant language online, but English-speaking culture imposes its references and values. This is demonstrated, among many other indicators, by the ranking of Shakespeare in Google queries—far ahead of Dante, Racine, or Goethe.

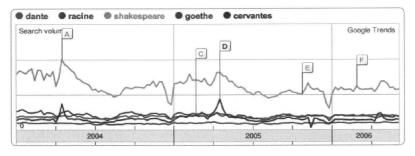

Rankings for some of the most famous European writers on Google Trends

A query of Google Book Search produces similar results. Does this indicate that search engines are agents of English imperialism? Of course not. These results simply demonstrate that English-speaking culture is (as of now) better served by the Internet than other cultures and that Google and other search engines present access to an unintentionally truncated and skewed culture.

Several factors contribute to this state of affairs. For one, the PageRank mechanism, which sorts documents according to the number and quality of links that point to them, puts those documents that attract the most attention at the top of the first page (as mentioned previously, the only place most Internet users look). Because English is used more than other European languages, the English documents show up at the top of results pages because they generate more hits than those written in other languages, which appear farther down the list. Thus, if I search for Goethe on Google.fr, I will find English documents before I find German ones.

This trend can only worsen because authors who want to be read may find it beneficial to use English rather than their native language. The phenomenon is a classic one, known as *ousting* or *crowding out*: The dominant language and culture tends to marginalize minority languages and cultures.* This phenomenon pervades the Internet. Copyright restrictions eliminate many works that are not accessible online, and if you can't read the text you want, you'll most likely turn to whatever is immediately accessible.

Corporate Data: A Comeback for Microsoft?

Another promising area of growth, *enterprise search*, is the searching of corporate intranets and file servers. Google's entrees into this area, Google Enterprise and the Google Search Appliance, would appear to pose no copyright problems and should not face cultural resistance, though they raise confidentiality issues. This area, however, highlights another obstacle to Google's growth: competition.

The competition is fierce in enterprise search, especially from Yahoo!'s OmniFind (in partnership with IBM) and Microsoft's Enterprise Search. Although as of this writing Microsoft holds only a pitiable third place in search (well under 9 percent, according to comScore.com), far behind Yahoo! (around 20 percent) and way behind Google (over 60 percent), considering the game is over would be a mistake.

Microsoft has many assets, not least of which is financial. Every year, they invest billions in research and development (R&D) alone.

---

* Entire aspects of world culture are never presented to the typical Internet surfer, so the fact that members of those cultures try to defend themselves is understandable. The solution would surely be a high-quality machine translator that can leap across linguistic borders, but obviously, that is a long way down the road. This phenomenon can have unexpected consequences, however—in the scientific disciplines, a curious reversal has resulted. In the past, working papers of scholarly articles were circulated only within the academic community, but today, anyone can read them on the Web. These working papers have become a more important source of information than the final articles that are published, after approval by peer review panels, in journals reserved for people with access to large university libraries.

While Microsoft has a very broad range of products that require considerable R&D, and like all large companies, it probably devotes a significant part of its budget to projects that will never get off the ground, the company still has a huge war chest.

Microsoft's second asset is its monopoly position. As an editor at *The Economist* pointed out, one can spend a day without using Google or any other search engine, but not using a Microsoft product is, for most us, impossible.

A third asset is Microsoft's determination. As Bill Gates enviously said in an interview, "Well, I have a meeting today with our people doing search. And that's an area where Google has got out in front, does a very good job. We're sort of the David vs. Goliath in that [chuckles] particular battle so we'll have fun talking to them about their progress."[25] Microsoft's leaders have never backed down from a contest. Many remember how they eliminated Netscape with Internet Explorer. Some think this matchup could be a repeat.

Google's domination of the enterprise search market is not a done deal. Microsoft knows more about business computing than Google, which could be an advantage. "Enterprise search is our business, it's our house and Google is not going to take that business," said Kevin Turner, chief operating officer of Microsoft.[26] Competition will be all the more intense because this market is large (Steve Ballmer, president of Microsoft, valued it at $13 billion). Dave Girouard, enterprise general manager at Google, readily acknowledges that nobody is ahead in this field.

Obviously, Google doesn't lack assets. Google has far more resources than Netscape had, not to mention the experience of employees and associates who worked for Netscape. It has a considerable lead in advertising and document management and more expertise in these areas than Microsoft. Also, Google has already signed agreements with some key players in business intelligence, like Cognos and Business Objects, that specialize in working with corporate data. Dell, the leading American distributor of PCs, supports Google, and so does Adobe; therefore, Google could benefit from companies that resent Microsoft's past bullying. But the battle is only beginning, and it promises to be all the more intense because corporate data processing is not a natural outgrowth of Google's business for these reasons:

- Most corporate data is stored in structured databases that current crawlers cannot effectively query or in formats that search engines don't handle.

- Many corporate files expire quickly or are updated versions of earlier documents.

- Corporate data is often dispersed among various machines, which makes access more difficult.

- Most companies are hierarchical organizations that limit access to information according to one's role in the organization.

This brings to mind the problems encountered when searching a PC for files stored on a hard drive. As most people will attest, the results usually contain a lot of "noise." Whoever can best solve this problem will carry the day.

The technical stakes are complex. Both Google's and MSN's search algorithms were designed for natural language queries of textual databases, so whether they will be able to query the numerical and formatted data found in traditional databases without making significant changes is uncertain. The crawlers they use were designed to index static pages, not dynamic ones that ask users to specify their query terms in search forms.

What's more, the thought process for enterprise search is somewhat different. In a textual database, a user starts with concepts and proceeds, through trial and error, by successive approximations. If the user doesn't find what he or she wants, the user modifies the query. This strategy is not best suited for corporate searches that look for precise data like a meeting date, an employee address, or regional sales figures. Using an algorithm like Google's will generate only noise.

But corporate data search is only a part of the story. The battle will also move to office automation tools where Microsoft has a monopoly and Google has ambition. The Google Docs Suite is Google's me-too Office product. Although rather mediocre when first released, Docs has evolved quickly and could become the standard suite of web-based office automation tools. This emerging market might also grow very quickly with the advent of *cloud computing*, in which software is provided "as a service" via the Internet.

Net Neutrality

Google's phenomenal growth has attracted many predators who want a piece of the action. Perhaps most alarming—and most threatening to Google—are the telecommunication companies that built the Internet's infrastructure. Without their telephone lines, the Web would not have been possible, so they are asking for a place at the table that they relinquished back in the mid-1990s. As long as the market remained relatively small, the large network operators let this go. After all, the Web brought them traffic. But now they want to pick up a new hand and get back into the game.

Their ambition is pretty simple: to install a toll system so Google and other major Internet players would have to pay to use their high-speed lines. No one would be denied access, but those that didn't pay would have slower access. This would, of course, limit the competition among content providers and give telephone and cable companies the ability to control how the Internet is used (and to discriminate among users).

Their principal argument is that they need to make major investments in the networks needed for distributing large-scale, Internet-based consumer services, like television, that require vast amounts of bandwidth. Google, Microsoft, Yahoo!, and others that want the Internet to remain "neutral" dispute their claims. If the telecom companies get their way, all big Internet players would have to share their advertising revenues with the "pipe merchants" to maintain a high level of service. This would end the dream of open exchange and would drastically change the Internet's economic model.

From a consumer point of view, the battle is between free access to all Internet content and network quality. When the Internet was mainly used for emailing or reading text, the speed and quality of the data stream was not a concern. That has all changed with the rise of the World Wide Web and the advent of new online services delivering music and video—services that demand a fast and uninterrupted data stream.

Fundamentally, net neutrality is about equal access to the Internet. As Eric Schmidt wrote in a letter to Google users in 2008, "The phone and cable monopolies, who control almost all Internet access, want the power to choose who gets access to high-speed lanes and whose content gets seen first and fastest. They want to build a two-tiered system and block the on-ramps for those who can't pay."[27]

The fight began on April 26, 2006, when the US House of Representatives rejected an amendment to prohibit discriminatory pricing for website suppliers. AT&T and Verizon scored an early victory, but discussions began immediately on the Web and in the blogosphere. Thousands of messages denounced the bill and encouraged people to inform the news media, the public, and their representatives. Self-proclaimed experts (some of whom really were experts) posted documents online that were as professional as those from any political PR agency.

This battle is extremely important, mixing economic principles with corporate interests, and it poses a serious challenge to Google's profitability. The fight is being played out in the corridors of the United States Congress and in quieter meetings of corporate boards of directors. Telephone and cable companies have vast resources and longstanding ties with legislators who aid them in their efforts to advance their agendas. The debates will be long, difficult, and highly technical, but these companies won't escape the scrutiny of informed public opinion.

One way to solve the problem might be to provide these operators with a share of advertising revenue by paying for some of their data assets, such as their customer base or the capabilities of their sales networks. But regardless of the solution, the eventual resolution is likely to decrease Google's profit.

Management: Overcoming Complexity

Winning these different fights won't be easy. But the principal challenges could well come from within Google itself. The main challenge is the business's increasing complexity, which can't be solved simply by hiring more staff. Google will also have to take the following things into account:

- Greater market diversity

- A richer commercial offering

- An increasing overlap of economic, political, and technical issues

- Technical problems that are extremely difficult to solve, like machine translation and the indexing of sounds and images

In 1955, Edith Penrose, an American economist (well known for her contribution to the resource-based view of strategic management) published a paper called "Limits to the Growth and Size of Firms" in *The American Economic Review*.[28] In this paper, she demonstrated that complexity limited the growth of companies. Beyond a certain point, she argued, executives no longer have sufficient cognitive capacity to deal with the mass of information they need to manage a company correctly. Furthermore, the availability or lack of top managerial and technical talent acts as the bottleneck for a firm's growth rate because "the services that the firm's resources will yield depend on the capacities of the men using them."

The history of corporate management tells us that the general solution to this problem has been one of more organization. Division of labor, specialization, the creation of multiple divisions, and decentralization have all been adopted to facilitate the management of more complex organizations. The question is, will Google's organizational model allow it to succeed, surrounded by these higher levels of complexity?

I think so, for these reasons:

- The Google triumvirate of Page, Brin, and Schmidt multiplies the cognitive capacities of the brain trust: Three leaders with clear roles can process more data, more quickly, than one.

- The rapid information flow throughout Google encourages teamwork, allows the organization to be reconfigured quickly, and allows projects that are unlikely to succeed to be terminated.

- Google's system of measurement provides engineers with direct information on user behavior and allows them to make quick and timely product development decisions. They don't have to wait for the results of marketing surveys or for instructions from a central planner—two major roadblocks to growth in aging, bureaucratic companies.

- Finally, Google's Swiss Army knife approach to product development has resulted in increasing numbers of new products because developers don't have to consider whether new products will integrate with existing ones. This approach gives Google the opportunity to test many new services simultaneously and, in the long run, could help it to expand its overall business without having to rely on only one service.

I'm not saying that Google can deal with every problem. The innovation machine that is so effective for smaller projects is probably not suited to solving the most complex problems like machine translation and content-based automatic image or video indexing. In this case, however, Google can hope that its strong relationship with the academic community will compensate for what might become a weakness.

Nor is it certain that Google's model is best suited to resolving the political problems that the company is likely to face, such as anti-trust questions. Like the issue of net neutrality, an anti-trust issue is more likely to be hashed out in Washington; engineers can't solve this problem.

On a more general note, can the company's business model itself hold up under sustained growth? Can the same methods that proved so efficient in a company with 5,000 employees be used a much larger company? Like most fast-growing companies, Google will not escape increased bureaucracy. The key to its success will be for Google to retain what made it a success in the first place: the rapid movement of ideas and sharing of information among its users, engineers, and leaders.

16

Like all fast-growing startups, Google has learned that the path of growth is littered with obstacles— shareholders who want to impose conventional management standards; customers, vendors, and staffers who complain about what they perceive as an anarchic atmosphere; executives stuck in the Peter Principle mold (in a hierarchy, every employee tends to rise to his level of incompetence); and obliging managers who forget that yesterday's victories don't always herald tomorrow's successes. None of these afflictions alone is usually fatal, but in general, they lead companies astray from the source of their originality and initial success. These are the risks of falling into conformist management.

In this chapter, I'll discuss some core issues that could affect Google's future, including pressure to limit free services, the temptation to become more bureaucratic, the downside of the innovation model, the development of class divisions among employees, and the unintended consequences of Google's compensation model.

The Danger of Free

Pressures for standardization come from all sides, and the company's economic model is the first target. Financial types regularly argue the benefits of Google's providing free services, whereas critics would prefer to see diverse income sources. But Google also faces pressure from unexpected skeptics, like Danny Sullivan, editor of *Search Engine Watch* and a leading technology expert, who wants Google to charge for its services for very different reasons. In a lampoon called "25 Things I Hate About Google," Sullivan pleaded with the company to charge users for putting content on the Internet in order to combat the rise of spam and noise:

> Stop giving away Blogger for free. It's just full of junk. Junk, junk, junk. If you let anyone have it with no barriers, surprise, some are going to take it and do bad things with it. . . . Charge people even a token amount ($1 even), and that will be a big barrier. Who's going to ding you for charging a $1 start-up fee that you can levy through Google Payments? If you must give it away for free, find a better, more trusted mechanism to partner with schools or others. Or make all Blogger blogs banned from being spidered for the first 30 days and open them up after that upon review. If that's not perfect, then figure something else out. But do something.[1]

Outside pressure for Google to change its economic model may be relatively discreet today, but this criticism is likely to become more strident as the growth of Google's revenues and benefits slows down. What if, in response to these pressures, Google begins charging for its free services?

Recall from Chapter 14 that Google has an implicit pact with its users. This symbiosis, as I've noted, has created a spirit of volunteerism. Instead of complaining when a product is deficient, users do everything they can to fix and improve it.

This paradigm has led to the growth of a network of partners who develop applications based on Google tools—for free. *Free* is the operative word behind so much of Google's success. And while prior to Google's launch, you might have argued that the availability of freely searchable information would lower the overall quality of information on the Internet, with authors holding their best work for the commercial sector, the exact opposite has proven true. Free access has supported a profusion of quality information of all sorts.

Several mechanisms are at play, including people who want to be published but can't find a publisher, the desire to revive books or articles that have "died" and become inaccessible because they are out of print, and most important, the personal pleasure of expressing opinions. In an article that deserves to be more widely disseminated, the economist Albert Hirschman explains that expressing opinions is in itself a source of well-being.[2] By indexing the Web for free, search engines have given everyone the opportunity to research, publish, and disseminate their opinions, and that reward is what drives much of Google's success. Like the potlatch discussed in Chapter 2, Google's is a gift economy, and if Google begins charging for those gifts, it risks breaking its own paradigm and losing its volunteers.

Still, providing free services has disadvantages. Beyond financial criticisms and Danny Sullivan's concerns about spam, if Google continues to offer its services for free, it could be forced to ration them, as it did with Gmail and Page Creator (a tool to help users build their own websites).

Rationing resources can be done in several ways, including first-come, first-served, by geographical area, and by invitation only. Each method has its advantages, but none is really satisfactory. Giving preference to those who show up first favors the users who are best informed and most loyal; sending out invitations supports the development of a black market, as Google learned with the introduction of Gmail. Before long, some users will become frustrated and disappointed and consider switching to a similar product made by another company. Thus, rationing can facilitate the emergence of competitors who are drawn into the market vacuum and can create permanent disaffection among excluded customers.

By giving away services, Google also deprives itself of information. As the Nobel Prize laureate Friedrich Hayek said, "The price system [is] a mechanism for communicating information."[3] Prices give buyers information about the relative availability and production cost of items they want to buy while, at the same time, giving sellers information on the extent to which consumers like a product or find it useful. Without this information, the company needs another way to determine consumer preferences. Communities of highly motivated users and a well-developed measurement system can mitigate this deficiency but may not entirely eliminate it.

This problem appeared when Google decided to remove some of its services in early 2009 because, as a Google blog put it, they were not "as popular as some of our other products."[4] But what does that say? How do you measure the success of a free service? By the number of users? Market share? You may subscribe to a newspaper you don't read every day simply because you want it to stay alive or because you know you might need the information that it publishes in the future. Use does not always convey information on usefulness: People rarely use public pay-phones, but sometimes they need them. The same could be true of some of Google's products.

Free services might also present unforeseen problems. When asked about the company's growth, Eric Schmidt always cites three factors: increases in traffic, increases in sales, and international growth in Europe and Asia. When pressed further and asked which of these factors propels growth, he says he doesn't know—that's very complicated to figure out—but all factors are moving forward. Then he adds that the areas with the greatest traffic increase are not necessarily those where sales grow fastest. That seems to make sense, but what will happen if traffic increases faster in Asia than in Europe while advertising sales grow faster in Europe than in Asia? Will the company subsidize Asian traffic with European income? Will it use the differential in growth rates to smooth out variations in its different markets? Or will it agree to act as a public utility in the smaller advertising markets?

Pressures to change Google's economic model will remain weak and divided as long as the company continues to earn money, but they will become stronger if profits decrease. When they do, Google's co-founders should be careful not to kill what made it successful in the first place.

I've already discussed the way that Google set up a two-tier voting system when the company went public in order to resist pressure from the financial markets. But with so many employee stock options, the company will also have to contend with internal pressures. If employees see their share value dropping because Google is neglecting the financial markets, they might pressure their leaders into conformism. The triumvirate may well prove particularly effective in this case, because convincing three leaders will be much more complicated than having to convince just one.

Organized Chaos and Bureaucratic Temptation

When companies grow, maintaining the informal lines of communication that make small organizations so adaptable becomes more difficult, and frail managerial hierarchies are easily overwhelmed. In response, bottleneck procedures are installed to try to make things run smoothly, but these procedures only limit a company's responsiveness and multiply burdensome administrative chores. Google is not immune to this phenomenon, and some developers have already begun to complain.*

Contractors who work for Google talk about anarchy, although seasoned employees call it *organized chaos*, which is not all that different. The lack of structural clarity seen in all fast-growing companies is, at Google, worsened by the blur of responsibilities. The crossover of employee skills and responsibilities may be highly effective for product development, but it becomes counterproductive when everyone has a say in everything.

Not knowing who is in charge of what, potential business partners, customers, and users begin to address their communications anywhere and everywhere. They clog the mailboxes of this person and that indiscriminately, and the company risks missing

---

* See, for instance, Kevin J. Delaney, "Start-Ups Make Inroads with Google's Workforce," *The Wall Street Journal*, June 28, 2007, *http://online.wsj.com/article/SB118299113663550893.html*.

opportunities and deadlines. The absence of a lawyer to defend a lawsuit in Belgium and the company's failure to renew its German domain name in early 2007 (which greatly amused the press) are only two examples of the dysfunction within an organization that has grown very quickly.

Rapid growth and size alone can also produce an environment that supports cheating. Imagining how employees might abuse the 20 percent rule doesn't take an expert. With few controls on their activities, workers can easily take advantage of this perk and spend more than 20 percent of their time on personal endeavors.

In fact, this appears to have already occurred. A study of working time ordered by management shows that engineers generally devote 30 percent of their time to personal projects. As a result, Google could fall victim to the same disease that struck PARC during the 1980s. The renowned Xerox research center invented the modern human–machine interfaces, document transfer languages, and several other breakthroughs, but none of these inventions was useful to a photocopier manufacturer. Brilliant, yes, but useful to the organization funding the work? No.

As with PARC, staff increases at Google will also increase the number of research projects that won't be integrated into the company's product line. So what will those engineers do with their pet projects once they've been turned down and work is no fun any more? If they have made a lot of money from their Google stock, maybe they'll go elsewhere to develop their applications and sell them back to Google one day. That would be in keeping with an old Silicon Valley tradition, but such a development would throw a little sand in the gears of Google's innovation machine.

Other potential risks with Google's current design include effort duplication and unproductive competition among teams—a situation that often occurs in research laboratories. Although competition is useful when it contributes to the progress of knowledge, it becomes counterproductive when teams work on parallel projects. Like other companies, Google can't market two spreadsheets, three word processors, or four mapping programs.

Growth naturally leads to the development of a denser, more complex, more hierarchical organization with clearly defined lines of authority and more traditional processes of control. Technology-based coordination at Google has delayed this progression toward increased bureaucracy so far, but how much longer will that last? Even technology-based coordination has proven to be effective when used in an average-sized company. Will it continue to work in one that employs several thousand people with branches around the world? Is there a threshold beyond which this coordination will become counterproductive?

When the Innovation Machine Sputters

Google's systematic release of new products as beta versions keeps things innovative and fresh and allows Google to outpace its competition. But even the best things can come to an end. Leaving products in beta for too long, especially if doing so results in Google's keeping decidedly mediocre products online, can be risky. Google might have plenty of reasons for waiting to remove a weak beta product; after all, if even a weak product satisfies a few hundred thousand users, why improve or remove it?

By releasing early but not finishing products, Google tips its hand to its competitors, revealing market needs and opportunities that other companies will try to fill. As a result, Google loses a competitive advantage and strengthens the competition. Still another very significant risk is that too many mediocre, unfinished products risk diluting Google's core of exceptional products, thus lowering its reputation and market penetration. Instead of securing a dominant position in each niche, Google could end up with a fragmented product line that distracts from the core business. Companies have finite resources, and when launching a new product, a company risks neglecting its existing products.

And let's not forget that Google is not invincible. As the sample statistics in the following table show (compiled in 2008 by Internet market experts), Google does not dominate all web markets.

As with all statistical data, caution is advisable here; there's no telling how accurate these percentages are. The methods used by Hitwise or comScore are not necessarily scientific, and other studies might give different results.

Market Share of Internet Services

Internet Service	Product	US Market Share
Email services (Source: Hitwise, February 2008)	Yahoo! Mail	54.63%
	Windows Live Mail	22.54%
	Gmail	5.51%
Search engines	Google	65.98%
	Yahoo! Search	20.94%
	MSNBC	6.90%
Maps (Source: Hitwise, January 2008)	MapQuest	50.25%
	Google Maps	22.20%
	Yahoo! Maps	13.34%
Video (Source: comScore, July 2008)	Google Sites	44.0%
	Fox Interactive Media	3.9%
	Yahoo! Sites	2.5%

Sources: Hitwise and comScore, 2008

Granted, the value of the competing products shown in the table aren't equal, and each grouping is at different stages in its lifecycle. Still, as this data shows, Google is not without competition—and very strong competition in certain markets.

Products That Work Are Sticky

One challenge that Google will continue to face in the Internet world is that products are sticky, especially when they get the job done reasonably well. Customers tend to continue using familiar products even when a new, better product comes along. Being first to market pays, even if first isn't always best. If someone has been using MapQuest for years, or even Yahoo! Maps for that matter, that person is likely to visit his old, familiar service when looking for directions. The tried and true is safe and easy, and people don't always want to put the additional effort into using a new tool like Google Maps, even if the tool is more powerful than its competitors.

Video and mapping products might escape this problem because users access them through a search engine, but the problem might prove to be much more complex for social media, networking sites, blogs, and webmail. For example, although many consider Gmail

Approach Web Statistics with Caution

Several companies specialize in analyzing online market share, such as Alexa, comScore, Nielsen Net Ratings, and Hitwise. The data used for their analysis is typically collected from user panels or ISPs. Each method gives different results and comparing one study to the other is hard because each panel's size and composition varies from one company to the other. Getting precise information on the methodology used in each study is difficult, and in addition, the techniques used to build these panels rarely prevent bias. Additionally, geographical factors are often ignored. This latter point is significant because some products are popular in one market but not in another. For example, Orkut, Google's social networking product, although relatively unpopular in the United States, is very well established in Brazil and Asia. For these reasons, approach statistics about the Web and its uses with caution. The statistics certainly suggest trends, but their accuracy can be questionable.

to be a more powerful webmail client than Windows Live Hotmail, Google has been unable to dislodge Hotmail. Inertia is certainly at work, but so is practicality: People are reluctant to change an email address because they don't want to bother informing everyone they know and the companies they do business with.

NOTE   *This resilience of inferior earlier technologies is no surprise. Anyone interested in innovation realized a long time ago that the best product doesn't always win, as Apple's fans know only too well. Economists have written a lot on the subject ever since they noticed that the QWERTY keyboard was not the best one available.[5]*

Finally, and most troubling for Google, these statistics are a reminder that the Swiss Army knife approach to product development does not guarantee success. As far as I can tell, Google's domination of the search market doesn't ensure market domination in other areas. Yes, the Google brand is extremely powerful, but branding alone won't make customers change products.

In this sense, Google is in a far less favorable position than Microsoft, which over the years has learned how to "trap" its customers into using multiple Microsoft products whether because of product integration or because customers like that familiar Microsoft interface. Microsoft excels in this area and is not shy about exerting its dominance. Google seems reluctant to use its power in the same way—a fact that many find appealing but one that may hinder the company's ability to compete as effectively in many areas. Google's Swiss Army knife approach to product development is unique, but this approach also has a strategic downside: It prevents Google from using a dominant market position to lead in other markets. Is that a flaw? Maybe for Google shareholders it is, but certainly not for champions of free market competition.

Human Resources: The Other Side of the Coin

Google's approach to human resource management has contributed greatly to its ability to attract and keep high-quality staff in an industry that experiences extremely high turnover (often more than 20 percent a year). But will its HR model last?

Google faces two risks that must be watched more closely: the risk of creating a caste system within the company and the risk linked to the unintended consequences of Google's compensation policy. I mentioned previously that engineers can devote 20 percent of their time to personal projects but sometimes use more. This attractive perk is reserved for engineers exclusively—and for good reason. Administrative or sales personnel would have a difficult time developing personal projects that would interest the company or the industry.

Google's founders were also liberal about issuing stock options to their early employees since the company couldn't pay competitive salaries then. Many of these early employees quickly became multimillionaires. Those who were hired later didn't get the same opportunity. Add in the fact that the company relies heavily on subcontractors and temps, and you can foresee an emerging caste system. Organizations of this type exist in they world, and they generally function without too many clashes. Hospitals follow the same model with classifications for doctors, nurses, and administrative staff. Administrators don't care for patients, and nurses rarely become doctors. So a caste system can endure in a hospital without creating problems. One main difference though is that hospital employees know what to expect. Hospitals have been around for a long time, and the class system that exists is well known and generally accepted.

But Google has not been around for a long time, and preventing conflicts from arising among spoiled engineers and administrators or salespeople who don't enjoy the same advantages could prove difficult. All employees are under heavy pressure to perform, but they don't all get the same privileges. As long as the company enjoys continued success, these frustrations will be of little importance, but tensions are more likely to build during difficult times (see Chapter 17 for more discussion of this).

To remedy some of these problems, in 2007 Google implemented a *transferable stock option (TSO)* program that allows employees to sell vested options in an online auction. The TSO gives employees a way to better control their total compensation, diversify their assets, and reduce the uncertainty of their stock options. By making employees a bit less sensitive to Google's share price, management may also be able to prevent employees from joining with shareholders to pressure management when it makes decisions that don't please the markets.

Google's ranks of millionaires (and billionaires, as shown in the following table) may also become another source of dissent and class division. Since companies have integrated stock options and share distributions into their employment packages, some top executives have become so rich that many consider it obscene. In the case of Google, this enrichment has grown to unusual proportions. For example, in February 2005, Wayne Rosing, David Drumond, George Reyes, Jonathan Rosenberg, Omid Kordestani, and others each made tens of millions of dollars by selling shares. Since then, most have added to those windfalls. Not a month goes by without someone selling his or her shares. By the end of this same year, Google employees had sold shares worth some $3 billion. That's a lot of wealth for a select group of employees.

Yes, I know these are legitimate earnings. The distribution of stock options to upper-level employees is nearly universal in the United States today. Of the top 500 American companies, 94 percent distribute stock to their executives, which counts for about half of their total remuneration. Those selling stock options today were there at the beginning, and they worked hard. They're happy to benefit from the company's generous policies toward its original employees. We can, however, wonder about the consequences of these massive sales (see the following table).

Stock Sales from July 2004 through January 2009

Employee	Money Earned from Stock Option Sales
Sergey Brin	$2,232,493,974
Lawrence Page	$2,192,202,709
Eric Schmidt	$1,684,288,451
Omid Kordestani	$1,337,070,606
John Doerr	$848,925,221

Source: Sec Form 4[6]

The distribution of huge blocks of shares has always posed a problem for economists concerned about the proper functioning of the stock exchange. Not that they're hostile to this distribution. On the contrary, they are sensitive to the arguments of those who see this as a way to reward top executives and encourage them to make decisions that benefit shareholders (although this argument may be losing favor, given the market today). The reasoning is simple: These managers will be concerned about the interests of the company's "owners" because they *are* owners with a large vested interest.

But economists also see risks. How do you prevent employees from making profits by using their knowledge of the company—including its development projects and its weaknesses—to grow rich at the expense of other less-informed shareholders? Imagining the foul plays unscrupulous leaders could devise is not hard. As one example, all they need to do is to sell their shares the day before the announcement of poor results to profit at the expense of investors who don't have this same information. Of course, insider trading is illegal in all developed countries. To prevent it without prohibiting stock options, American and European stock exchange authorities require that employees submit a disclosure statement whenever they sell shares in the company they work for. They must state in advance the numbers of shares, dates, and possibly the minimum price per share required for the sale.

This requirement was devised by American stock exchange authorities to avoid cheating, but how effective is it? Does it prevent corporate leaders from repeating the rapacious swindles that have caused so many scandals? According to Alan D. Jagolinzer, an economist at Stanford University who analyzed actual sales by employees at 180 companies from 2001 to 2003, sales of stock options were concentrated within the most favorable periods, and stock performances were mostly better than they should have been.[7] Changing dates and sales volumes might be difficult, but nothing prevents executives from manipulating corporate communications. So a CEO who already announced the sale of a large block of stock on May 15 can set up an announcement that is designed to increase the stock price a few days before the date.

An analysis of stock sales by Google leaders doesn't indicate any manipulations of this sort, even if the sales were concentrated on the most favorable days of the month. But beyond the possibility of cheating, unloading stock options at this rate is surprising. The volume of these sales is so large that concern about their cumulative impact on the markets is valid. When some 8 percent of a company's total worth changes hands within a few months, could that depress the stock price? And if that were the case, wouldn't the external shareholders have a right to protest? Many observers saw a signal of doubt here: If the top executives sell the stocks they hold, maybe they are wary of the company's ability to sustain the same rate of growth. So these sales might send negative signals to the market.

Looking more closely, however, these sales are less surprising than they might appear at first glance. The early sale of stock options to take profits is currently a common practice among managers. The same people who swear by taking risks when making decisions for the company avoid those risks when it comes to their personal welfare. This is sound thinking: They don't want to put all their investments into one company. Their financial advisors recommend diversifying their assets. But psychological factors also come into play. Do they know the company better and see its limitations? Employees are usually more sensitive than investors to the company's risks and vulnerabilities. They often underestimate the value of stock options and cash them in instead of taking money out of a savings account.

Companies don't take offense at this; they put up with it and see it as a way to anticipate when an employee is planning to leave.

I should add that these sales don't modify the balance of power within the board of directors. At the outset, Sergey Brin and Larry Page got shares with multiple voting rights that guaranteed their control of the company. This mechanism allows them to sell large stock volumes without losing any influence.

These stock sales could even be rationalized as being useful. Stock options motivate leaders to make decisions that will excite shareholders and make them feel that everything is being done to ensure growth and share price increases. In fact, authors who have examined this form of remuneration in detail have shown that managers with most of their personal capital invested in the company they work for tend to behave cautiously; they don't want to lose everything in a lawsuit filed by irate stockholders. In this context, the sale of option shares can be good for the company, its shareholders, and its employees. By sheltering part of a young fortune from the fluctuations of stock market prices, a leader relieves himself or herself of market pressures. The leader can take more risks since he or she has less to lose; the leader can also invest for the long term since his or her own future is already assured.

Although these massive sales don't present every concern that has been raised, others do exist. For one, when employees get rich, behavior quickly changes, including the behavior of those who have become rich and those who haven't. Motivation may suffer, and whereas complacency and arrogance among some may arise, jealousy and resentment may arise in others. Conflicts of interest can also occur. Once you own a dream mansion, the latest Ferrari, a second home, and maybe a private jet (as Eric Schmidt does), you need to find something to do with your money. Many donate to charitable organizations; others invest in startups, becoming business angels. But conflicts of interest might arise when a former employee funds a startup whose business competes directly with one of Google's business activities—a risk that increases as Google expands its business lines.

Aside from that, how can you avoid abuses? Investing in a startup is a little like playing poker. With luck, you might win a lot; with less luck, you might lose everything. Even if you are financially set for the rest of your life, losing is never fun. Might one of these business angels be tempted to recycle one of the companies he or she financed by selling it to Google at a highly inflated price? Who knows if they can all resist the temptation?

Pressure from shareholders and partners, dysfunction, corruption, and the aging of people and organizations are powerful forces that drive companies to conform and normalize the original model that worked so well. Google is not immune to these forces, but it benefits from counterforces as well. I have cited the executive triumvirate and technology-based coordination as two examples. To that I add a third: the mechanism of reputation-based control. As long as these three mechanisms remain in place, Google's model will endure. The model will evolve and change to better meet the constraints of a more demanding environment, but it will persist.

Of course, things would be different if one of these three pillars were to suddenly collapse. The company would then be condemned to drift toward a hierarchical bureaucratic model with its superimposed layers of managers and the systems of rigid control and planning found at all large companies.

17

A LOOK AHEAD

As I write this chapter, we are in the midst of a global economic crisis that, since mid-2008, has dramatically affected the economies of all developed countries. These unusual economic circumstances, not seen in recent memory, provide an opportunity to question the strength of the Google model and its ability to weather an economic recession.

Many people remember the economic downturns of the early 1990s and early 2000s, but since the 1930s and the Great Depression, many other recessions have occurred. The National Bureau of Economic Research (NBER), which keeps track of such economic events, has identified a dozen recessions in the United States alone. These crises are more or less serious and deep, but all share certain traits. Specifically, they do the following:

- Destroy corporate value through a sharp fall in share prices

- Cause less competitive companies to disappear

- Lead to reduced spending on activities that do not promise immediate return, such as advertising, marketing, and R&D

- Cause companies to restructure in order to seek productivity gains

- Result in the adoption of defensive strategies such as price reductions, which ultimately weaken the most vulnerable companies

In long crises, these manifestations become self-fulfilling: Cuts in spending and layoffs contribute to massive unemployment and lower prices that undermine business. And last but not least, these crises give rise to what Joseph Alois Schumpeter, an Austrian economist famous for his analysis of business cycles, calls a "process of creative destruction," in which old ways of doing things are destroyed and replaced by new technologies and management methods.[1]

Not surprisingly, the longer an economic crisis lasts, the greater its effects. After a recession, the economic landscape is generally very different from what it was before, and we have no reason to expect that things will be any different this time. Some companies will disappear, others will rise to new heights, and several markets will change radically. These changes will be true not only of the automotive and financial industries but also of advertising and retail, two markets of direct importance for Google.

This chapter will assess the current recession's potential impact on Google. First, I'll examine the recession's impact on Google's business environment and new opportunities. Next, I'll examine the impact of the measures that Google has begun to take in response to this crisis as I explore questions such as whether Google will change its management model (and if does, how) and whether the recession will solve the business problems generated by Google's rapid growth before the crisis occurred. Finally, I'll examine whether Google's unique managerial model is likely to be more or less effective under these circumstances than more traditional ways of doing business.

Less Innovation Results in Less Competition

One of the first victims of any financial crises is innovation. R&D is one of the first areas that companies cut in recessionary times. When companies don't cut R&D, they ask researchers to work on solutions to improve productivity rather than create innovative products.

This reduction in innovation is evidenced by the reduction in the number of patents filed during economic recessions. For example, as you can see in the following graph, in 1996, following the 1995 recession, the number of patents filed decreased by nearly 15 percent. In this case, the decline in patent applications was short-lived and patent activity returned to normal in subsequent years, but in a very long depression, this assumption can't be made. For example, patent filings collapsed in 1929 and did not resume in earnest until World War II.

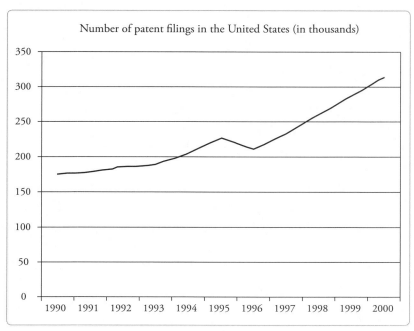

Number of patent filings in the United States (in thousands)

Source: United States Patent and Trademark Office[2]

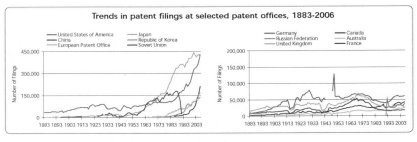

Trends in patent filings at selected patent offices, 1883-2006

Source: World Intellectual Property Organization[3]

This drop in patent activity is further confirmed by a study conducted on the chemical and pharmaceutical industries in Great Britain and Germany, two industries that contribute heavily to R&D expenditures. "In the replies to the questionnaire we sent managers," explain its authors, "61% of the respondents indicated that R&D spending has been decreased during the early 1990s, and 66% said that less R&D personnel were hired. In addition, 39% indicated that the focus of R&D had changed, and 33% mainly sought more cooperation to fight cost."[4]

One reason for the decline in expenditures is that many companies base their R&D budget on past sales. If sales are weak in a preceding year, R&D expenses will be cut in the following year and vice versa. Another explanation is, of course, that many companies disappear during these periods.

Nor does this phenomenon spare the most innovative industries. For example, as shown in the following graph, the bursting of the Internet bubble during the early 2000s had an impact on patent applications in the IT industry as well—an industry known for its history and emphasis on innovation.

In the IT sector, this situation could be aggravated by the financial crisis's impact on one of its major sources of funding: venture capital. You can probably imagine how reducing the availability of venture capital could result in the pace of innovations decreasing as young, cash-strapped companies are forced to cut their R&D budget for lack of needed funds.

Like all investors, venture capitalists are naturally more demanding in difficult times. As one such venture capitalist, Will Price of

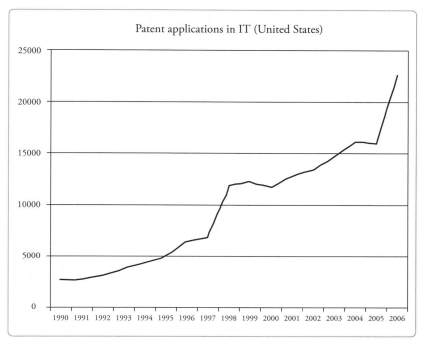

Patent applications in IT (United States)

Source: United States Patent and Trademark Office[5]

Hummer Winblad,[*] explains on his blog: "With a lack of good exits, why would a VC want to invest in a company?"[6] Even those who would like to take advantage of circumstances may not for lack of an opportunity to get a significant return on their investment.

The reduction of R&D budgets is likely to have the following consequences:

- Companies whose business model is too fragile or who still rely on venture capitalists to finance their growth could disappear.

- Second-rate players are likely to limit or even abandon their research efforts to focus on their core business.

- Innovative firms lacking in financial resources may seek the protection of more powerful firms, whether through partnerships or outright mergers.

---

* Funded in 1989, Hummer Winblad Venture Partners was the first venture capital fund to invest exclusively in software companies.

The upshot is that the recession is likely to raise the bar for entry into the market, thus reducing the likelihood that new competitors will emerge with ideas that could threaten dominant firms. At the same time, the recession gives larger firms the chance to buy companies cheaply. All of this is likely to benefit Google, allowing it to solidify its strength in many markets and giving it an opportunity to take over competitors in markets, like social networking, that it has failed to win.

The Impact on the Advertising Market

Recessions put a crimp on R&D spending, but they really do a number on advertising budgets, which are highly sensitive to changes in economic cycles. According to Robert G. Picard, considered by many to be the father of media economics, a decrease of 1.15 percent in the gross domestic product, a measure of national income, leads to an average decrease of 5.98 percent in advertising budgets, as illustrated in the following graph.[7]

While the strength of the correlation between recessions and advertising spending differ among countries (from very strong in Germany, Finland, the United Kingdom, France, and the United States to almost nonexistent in Japan), the correlation will be significant in Google's main markets. Clearly, Google's advertising

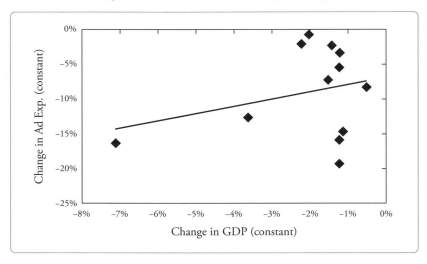

Effect of change in GDP on advertising expenditures (Source: Robert G. Picard)[8]

revenues are likely to be directly affected by the global recession, which threatens Google's business model.

To assess the impact of the world's economic crisis on Google's advertising revenues, consider the evolution of online advertising and its impact on user behavior and the price of keywords. In 2008, as has been true at the beginning of every major recession, several large corporations like Coca-Cola and Visa and many automobile manufacturers and banks announced reductions in their advertising budgets. As large advertisers, their decision sent shockwaves throughout the industry.

Cuts in the advertising budgets of small and medium enterprises don't make the front page, but they can significantly impact major media.* But how will these cuts in advertising spending affect web-based advertising? In difficult times, advertisers are more concerned about the costs and direct results of their advertising campaigns. This quest for results and concern with efficiency should benefit those advertising vehicles that offer their customers ways to better control and measure their campaign's effectiveness. Seen from this point of view, web-based advertising, especially on a search engine like Google, should suffer less than advertising in traditional media.

Google may well benefit from the redirection of advertising budgets as corporations increase online advertising. According to a study published by McKinsey & Company in 2007, online advertising is likely to grow significantly over the next few years:

- Only 69 percent of firms interviewed use online media advertising very frequently.

- Only 30 percent of companies that do use online media spend more than 10 percent of their budget on this new advertising vehicle. But that percentage is expected to change quickly: "Three years from now twice as many respondents believe they will be spending at least that much online, and 11 percent say they will be spending the majority of their budgets online."[9]

---

* According to a study conducted by BDO Seidman, one-third of chief marketing officers at leading US retailers said that their marketing and advertising budgets have been reduced after the financial market meltdown (BDO Seidman, 2008 Holiday Marketing Release, December 2008).

The main obstacle to this market's development could be the lack of appropriately skilled personnel: Success in this new media demands a skill set not necessarily found in traditional advertising departments.

Of course, Google is not the only player in the online advertising game. For example, according to the same McKinsey survey, although considered to be the most effective form of online advertising, search engine advertising occupies third place (behind email and banner advertising) in online advertising budgets. But the balance is likely to shift quickly: Seventy-one percent of respondents said that their budgets for search engine advertising would increase. The recession is unlikely to make them change their mind.

Shrinking advertising budgets should also give Google, the search engine leader, an advantage because companies are likely to concentrate most of their effort on the one company that provides them with the greatest visibility. As a corollary, this shift could hinder the development of alternative online advertising venues like the social networks, Facebook, MySpace, and similar sites.

The Rise of eCommerce

When times are tough, consumers price shop. And what better way to price shop than with a search engine like Google? But electronic commerce is still only in its infancy. According to the US Census Bureau, in 2008 online shopping accounted for less than 5 percent of all retail shopping.[10] This surprisingly small number leaves a large margin for growth.

The growth of eCommerce is naturally friendly to search engines since consumers turn to them when looking for a product online. For example, a Performics study conducted in 2007 showed that 70 percent of US mothers who shop online price-shop online before purchasing, and 57 percent shop online before purchasing in a brick-and-mortar store.[11] Why is online price-shopping good for Google? Because whenever consumers search for products online via Google, Google serves them ads.

In addition, electronic commerce gives search engines the opportunity to develop new services and new revenue sources. Google could monetize YouTube, for example, with eCommerce, as it offers advertisers a way to raise product awareness. Further, Google Product Search (a price comparison service), Google Base (a database that can be used by companies to sell products), and Google Checkout (a payment service) all offer Google ways either to sell advertising directly or to collect a commission on transactions. These are additional growing sources of revenue that may well benefit from a recession as consumers do more shopping and buying online.

Traffic Is Not Revenue

But the global recession poses a risk as well. Consider the fact that Google gets its income from selling keywords at auction. For these revenues to grow, the number of clicks on ads tied to keywords must increase and the price of keywords rise. Neither of these can be inferred from an increase in the number of visitors.

The value of keywords depends on several factors. First, of course, competition among advertisers is important: The more advertisers desire a particular word, the more that word's price increases. But the value also depends on an advertiser's skills (poorly chosen words do not generate clicks), on his or her strategies (those who use web advertising to build or protect their brand are more interested in impressions than clicks), and on the advertiser's financial resources; obtaining information on competitor bids is difficult, so wealthy advertisers may bid high to outbid the competition.

The financial turmoil could change all this by reducing competition and the propensity of large firms to use advertising as a way to build their brand. The recession could force larger firms to optimize their spending and pay more attention to ad performance. In fact, Google's keyword auction system could conspire to make things more financially difficult under these circumstances: Unlike other methods of price setting that ensure a certain stability (what economists call *price stickiness*), auctions respond quickly to the slightest changes in user behavior and economic conditions.[12]

One of the first effects of this sensitivity to economic conditions is the seasonality of the *cost per keyword*, a ratio that combines the cost per click with the volume of clicks and that represents the average cost of purchasing a keyword for an entire month. For example, according to Performics, cost per keyword rose to around $55 in December 2005 from approximately $26 at the end of August 2005.[13] Although this seasonality was concealed by Google's rapid revenue growth, seasonality might increase in this recession. Could this cause a problem for Google's cash flow? Cash flow is usually the greatest challenge for companies that experience large seasonal fluctuations. Google is, of course, a special case, but increased seasonality could encourage its managers to strengthen their investment in activities than can be monetized by means other than advertising (like cloud computing, for example, which we will discuss shortly) in order to level out cash flow.*

Recessions: A Time to Reorganize

During financial crises and recessions, companies reduce their costs, restructure, and streamline their organization. Some restructure because they are forced to; others restructure simply to take advantage of the situation. Two factors contribute to these moves:

- Employees afraid to lose their jobs accept measures they would have fought otherwise, such as pay cuts, reduced work weeks, and reduced benefits.

- The production slowdown gives firms the opportunity to invest in productivity-improving activities such as reorganization or training. As Robert E. Hall of Stanford University explains, "Measured output may be low during (recession) periods, but the time spent reorganizing pays off in its contribution to future productivity."[14]

In other words, the cost of productivity-improving activities falls. This trend could benefit Google and, more generally, companies that offer hosting solutions and software to reduce the costs associated with data processing.

---

* The seasonality of prices during recessions has been little researched, but the few studies on the subject seem to suggest that seasonality is more significant during these periods. See, for instance, Antonio Matas-Mir and Denise R. Osborn, "Does Seasonality Change Over the Business Cycle? An Investigation Using Monthly Industrial Production Series," University of Manchester, Center for Growth & Business Cycle Research, July 2003, Number 009, *http://www.ses.man.ac.uk/cgbcr/discussi.htm.*

Two areas seem particularly promising:

- Online office automation and collaboration tools (à la Google Docs) that can help reduce the cost of traveling and collaborating

- Cloud computing, a technology that allows the outsourcing of applications and data to the computers and networks of companies like Google, IBM, Microsoft, or Amazon.com

While companies are unlikely to port all of their applications to the Web and close all of their data centers (as some analysts once thought they would), this technology is likely to expand thanks to the financial crisis. Rather than abandoning expensive projects due to shrinking budgets, IT departments will be able to implement these projects without investing scarce financial resources. When cloud computing is used, investment capital can be replaced with operating expenses.

Like eCommerce, cloud computing offers Google the opportunity to find new income sources. However, Google's search market dominance will not help much in this new business. Google's lack of knowledge of large firms and their ERP tools and the lack of skills and staff in traditional IT and consulting services could be real obstacles, especially in the face of competitors like IBM, HP, and Oracle. Nevertheless, Google still has a major asset in this market: its ability to manage, store, and analyze huge amounts of data.

Recessions: An Opportunity to Streamline

Google could be satisfied with these rather optimistic forecasts about its ability to survive the recession, but the company won't be idle. Google will take advantage of this recession to reorganize. As of this writing, Google has already announced several cost-cutting measures, including the following:

- Reducing the number of HR consultants and other temporary personnel

- Cutting employee benefits and perks

- Slowing new staff recruitment

- Simplifying its product line by removing duplicate products (such as Page Creator and Google Sites) and closing services that have not found their public (such as Lively or Datasets Research)

- Introducing advertising for new products such as Google Finance

In my opinion, Google's main efforts should focus on streamlining its procedures and its product range. Its rapid growth and acquisition pace has created a host of coordination problems that won't be solved by quickly expanding its administrative departments. The company is simply littered with too many projects, trying to do too many things with not enough overall coordination. The time has come for Google to better integrate its products, rethink and improve coordination among departments, and implement procedures for allocating budgets that take greater account of a project's profitability.

These changes are, for some, long overdue, but they are not without risk. They are likely to create tension within the company, not only between management and employees but also between the co-founders: Agreeing on spending cuts is much more difficult than agreeing on budget increases.

These cost-cutting moves may also negatively impact staff motivation and loyalty. Engineers may fear changes to the business model that would make Google "another boring big firm." New methods for allocating budgets based on profitability could also affect the very delicate balance between financial incentives and the personal rewards that come from the satisfaction of creating a great product or respect from peers (as discussed in Chapters 6 and 16).

This risk is made all the more real because the current economic crisis has deeply affected Google's wage models, which are based on stock options and profit sharing. The rapid decline of stock markets is forcing all major US companies to invent new ways to remunerate their employees, and Google won't be an exception.

The task won't be an easy one. Companies traditionally resist reducing wages during recessions for fear of reducing employee morale. As Truman Bewley explains in his book, *Why Wages Don't Fall During a Recession* (based on interviews with 300 business executives, labor leaders, and professional recruiters), "employers resist pay cuts largely because the savings from lower wages are usually outweighed by the cost of denting workers' morale. . . . Falling morale raises staff turnover and reduces productivity. Cheerier workers are more productive workers, not only because they work better, but also because they identify more closely with the company's interests. In other words, firms typically prefer layoffs to pay cuts because they do less harm to morale."[15]

Management: A Recession-Proof Model?

Google's management model is particularly unique among companies. The question is, will Google's management model help the company mitigate the consequences of a deep recession? And if so, how?

In order for any company's management to guide a business through a recession, management must be able to do the following:

- Adapt products and organization structure quickly to meet the changing demands of customers

- Reduce the impact of reorganization and staff cuts on employee morale and productivity

The way Google manages its products and innovation should help. The company should be able to adapt quickly to changing markets and the demands of its customers for these reasons:

- Thanks to Google's Swiss Army knife approach to product development, products can change quickly.

- The "release early and often" principle allows Google to adapt to users' expectations and amend its products as necessary.

- The use of open source solutions and Google's special relationship with users and developers facilitate the rapid integration of innovations.

Google's management structure, composed of small teams and lacking in hierarchy, should be an asset in difficult economic times. Its effectiveness is obvious when compared to what happens in companies that downsize. In a traditional hierarchical organization, downsizing means reduced promotion prospects, limiting management layers, and fewer career opportunities for everyone. But at Google, where much of one's job satisfaction is intrinsic and where improving one's reputation among peers is perhaps as important as improving one's position within the hierarchy, the chances of declining motivation due to downsizing are reduced.

Effective in good economic times, Google's management model should also help in economic downturns. Although its model does not eliminate the effects of a recession, it should limit them significantly and allow for a quick rebound, post-recession.

Google Post-Recession: Stronger but More Cautious

Google will probably resist this recession, and this period may give Google an opportunity to strengthen its dominant position in the market for online advertising and to create new revenue-producing services. Nevertheless, the economic crisis should remind Google that, despite its near-term successes, its economic model, based almost solely on advertising, is highly sensitive to economic changes. This time Google should get a pass, but that won't always be the case. Google needs to diversify its income sources in the same way that all major US companies did in the wake of the Great Depression.

The recession will force Google to rethink, restructure, and reorganize. Some efforts will be welcomed, but Google faces many risks. If clumsily implemented, the changes that Google will be forced to make to its business could create tension within the company and affect one of its most precious endowments: the morale of its employees and the goodwill that it has generated in the marketplace.

More than an exceptional personal and collective adventure, Google represents the invention of a new management model—and calling it revolutionary is no exaggeration. Analysis reveals some of the features that have distinguished other great industrial revolutions: the discovery of a mass market, the invention of products, the development of new techniques for marketing and staff management. Like every great management revolution, this one draws its legitimacy from the way it adapted to an economic, social, and cultural environment very different from that of companies formed during the 1970s and 1980s.

Technology plays a decisive part in all of this. You've seen throughout this book how Google put technology at the core of its management practices. Technology is used as a tool for internal coordination rather than hierarchical control; as an interface between the company and its customers and users; and of course, as the engine of its information system. But the integration of technology into management methods is only one aspect of this revolution. This revolution also has a social dimension. Rarely has any enterprise relied as much as Google on the "voluntary capital" of its workers, their contacts, and their relationships to test new products or to garner new ideas and enhance products. Undoubtedly, Google is the first company to have figured out how to benefit from the development of fan communities comprised not only of evangelists but also of observers and pitiless critics (Google's most effective information sources precisely because their criticism is so severe).

Google's repeated successes have created genuine enigmas for anyone interested in management strategy. To summarize just a few:

- Google has never spent a cent on advertising.

- The public is welcome to criticize the company.

- Google has no qualms about breaking every managerial rule in the book, refusing to observe even the most elementary marketing practices.

- For a long time, Google paid developers less than the competition—yet the company has attracted the best employees and kept them longer.

So how did Google become one of the world's best-known brands in only a few years? How did Google get away with all this?

Throughout this book, I have tried to answer these questions, among others, and I've attempted to explain the solutions Google has adopted to achieve these results. Yet taking these methods at face value and turning them into applicable recipes for every company and situation would be difficult. Bookstores are full of tomes that promise to teach the seven, eight, or ten "laws" or "steps" to success. Only the naïve would take them literally. Management has no more absolute laws than economics does. Or rather, as soon as you think you've found a law, another idea comes along to contradict it instantly. This is predictable: No two companies are alike. Even those that closely resemble each other have their own unique history, work in different institutional contexts and economic environments, and thus do not fall under the same sets of constraints.

Nobody will create a successful company simply by copying Google. Managers would do better to ask the same questions Google's leaders asked themselves, with the goal of gaining insight wherever possible from Google's methods. Then they will need to adapt those methods to their own business in ways that meet their own challenges. Success in management, as in any other discipline, requires both work and imagination. Of course, innovation is where Google sets a real example. Of all the strategies its leaders instituted, the 20 percent rule is certainly the most surprising. Yet implementing it is easy wherever employees are asked to demonstrate creativity.

Industrial research laboratories come naturally to mind, but this principle can also be found in some of the strangest places, like a famous restaurant in southwestern France that earned two stars in the Michelin guide.* The chef has built his reputation on the originality of his cuisine and his ability to introduce new menu items regularly. Each month, he asks his sous-chefs to invent a new recipe during their working hours. These creations are tested by all the employees, the best are placed on an "experimental" menu board that is shown to the customers, and the most successful dishes make their way onto the main menu. The benefits of this approach are comparable to those that Google derives from the 20 percent rule: The chef can easily add new menu items without much risk; he attracts the best, most creative apprentices; and he improves his reputation in the medium of cuisine, which is the best way to satisfy both customers and critics.

Google's Swiss Army knife approach and beta releases of new products offer other solutions for complexity and uncertainty. I can safely say that Google's management model will spread throughout

---

* Michelin is quite stingy about awarding stars. In all of France, 620 restaurants have a single star; 70 have two stars; and only 26 are in the rarefied three-star category (2006 figures).

the world of software development. But beyond the benefits to the management of complexity, the Google model reduces delays in making decisions, delays that can affect the marketing of new products. Users participate in product design. One of Google's strong suits is its ability to revisit relationships with its users and customers.

Companies all claim they want to make the customer the centerpiece of the company. This claim has become one of the most current themes in management literature. But usually, the more they say it, the less they do it. Google shows that companies really can give users a higher priority by doing the following things:

- Giving the customer a voice in saying what price he or she is willing to pay through the AdWords bidding system.

- Collecting data on how its tools are used and by sharing this information with the people who design the products without filters or intermediaries. The marketing experts no longer dictate to engineers what users want; the users themselves dictate it through their daily actions.

- Drawing on employees' imagination and abilities to develop applications that look interesting. If IKEA revolutionized the world of furniture with the assemble-it-yourself approach, Google (and others, like Wikipedia) have given us a different model that puts intelligence at the service of every single individual.

But above all, keep this one thing in mind: When given a voice, customers will speak up. This prevents them from taking the alternative course, which is to go away.

Google can also be used as a model in the field of human resources. By emphasizing reputation, the company reevaluated social control and the intrinsic motivations too often neglected by traditional organizations: "I will work to fulfill my inner needs, to gain recognition, and to earn the respect of my colleagues." And yes, the vast majority of employees will do just that. This device simultaneously allows Google to reduce its hierarchical structure greatly, to retain employees who might have been tempted to look elsewhere, and to solve the recurring problem of finding a way to promote technicians who are highly skilled but don't necessarily have the personal qualities of good managers.

To manage innovation, human resources, products, and customer relations, Google's leaders looked at the problems all companies encounter from a new angle. They were able to define and simultaneously solve the problems of division of labor and specialization with distinguished results. They have managed to build a rich, complex model that serves not only as an example to emulate but also as a subject of study for anyone interested in corporate management.

NOTES

Chapter 1

1. Vannevar Bush, "As We May Think," *The Atlantic Monthly*, July 1945, 101–8.

2. Ibid.

3. Larry Page and Sergey Brin, "The Anatomy of a Large-Scale Hypertextual Web Search Engine," *Computer Networks and ISDN Systems* 30, no. 1–7 (April 1998).

4. Paul Gompers et al., "Skill vs. Luck in Entrepreneurship and Venture Capital: Evidence from Serial Entrepreneurs," NBER Working Paper Series No. 12592, 2006.

5. Ronald J. Gilson, "Corporate Governance and Economic Efficiency: When Do Institutions Matter?" *Washington University Law Quarterly* 74, no. 2 (1996): 327–45.

6. James Gleick, "Patently Absurd," *The New York Times Magazine*, March 12, 2000, 44–9.

7. "Letter from the Founders, 'An Owner's Manual' for Google's Shareholders," Form S-1 Registration Statement, April 29, 2004, i.

Chapter 2

1. Marcel Mauss, *The Gift: The Form and Reason for Exchange in Archaic Societies*, trans. W.D. Halls (New York: W.W. Norton & Company, 2000).

2. Robert B. Ekelund, Jr. and Robert F. Hebert, *Secret Origins of Modern Microeconomics: Dupuit and the Engineers* (Chicago: University of Chicago Press, 1999).

3. Stuart Elliott, "How Effective Is This Ad in Real Numbers? Beats Me," *The New York Times*, July 20, 2005.

4. Peter Coy, "The Secret to Google's Success," *BusinessWeek*, March 6, 2006, *http://www.businessweek.com/magazine/content/06_10/b3974071.htm*.

5. Joseph Weizenbaum, *Computer Power and Human Reason: From Judgment to Calculation* (New York: Penguin Books Ltd., 1984).

6. Byron Reeves and Clifford Nass, *The Media Equation: How People Treat Computers, Television, and New Media Like Real People and Places* (New York: Cambridge University Press, 1996).

7. Brendan Kitts and Benjamin Leblanc, "Optimal Bidding on Keyword Auctions," *Electronic Markets* 14, no. 3 (September 2004): 186–201.

8. Ben Charny, "Some Google Advertisers Cutting Spending," *MarketWatch*, January 3, 2007, *http://www.marketwatch.com/news/story/google-advertisers-cutting-spending-keyword/story.aspx?guid={E9B9CEA8-EA47-48C6-A91F-69F53F018AE2}*.

9. Chris Anderson, *The Long Tail: Why the Future of Business is Selling Less of More* (New York: Hyperion, 2006). See also Clay Shirky, "Power Laws, Weblogs, and Inequality," email to Networks, Economics, and Culture mailing list, February 8, 2003, *http://www.shirky.com/*, and Lada A. Adamic and Bernardo A. Huberman, "Zipf's Law and the Internet," *Glottometrics* 3 (2002): 143–150.

10. Rajeev Kohli and Raaj Sah, "Market Shares: Some Regularities," 2004, *http://www.economics.smu.edu.sg/events/Paper/Sah.pdf*.

11. Gal Oestreicher-Singer and Arun Sundararajan, "Recommendation Networks and the Long Tail of Electronic Commerce," (presented at the 27th International Conference on Information Systems, Milwaukee, WI, December 2006).

12. Catherine Tucker and Juanjuan Zhang, "How Does Popularity Information Affect Choices? Theory and A Field Experiment," MIT Sloan School Working Paper 4655-07, March 31, 2008.

13. Gavin O'Malley, "Marketers Threaten To Put Majority Of Budget Online," *MediaPost*, November 13, 2007, *http://www.mediapost.com/publications/index .cfm?fuseaction=Articles.san&s=70866&Nid=36310&p=411263*.

14. Eric Schmidt, quoted by Chris Anderson, "Google's Long Tail," *The Long Tail*, February 12, 2005, *http://www.longtail.com/the_long_tail/2005/02/ googles_long_ta.html*.

15. James Manyika, "Google's view on the future of business: An interview with CEO Eric Schmidt," *The McKinsey Quarterly*, September 2008, *http://www .mckinseyquarterly.com/Googles_view_on_the_future_of_business_An_interview_ with_CEO_Eric_Schmidt_2229*.

Chapter 3

1. Arijit Chatterjee and Donald C. Hambrick, "It's all about me: Narcissistic CEOs and their effects on company strategy and performance," *Administrative Science Quarterly* 52, no. 3 (2007): 351–86.

Chapter 4

1. Christopher Sacca, "Seriously, You Can't Touch This . . . ," *Chris Sacca's 'What is Left?'*, October 22, 2005, *http://www.whatisleft.org/lookie_here/2005/10/ index.html*.

2. Bill Gates, interview by David Allison, "Transcript of a Video History Interview with Mr. William "Bill" Gates," Microsoft Corporation, Bellevue, Washington, *http://americanhistory.si.edu/collections/comphist/gates.htm*.

3. Dr. John Sullivan, "A Case Study of Google Recruiting: Can Any Firm Compete Against This Recruiting Machine?" May 12, 2005, *http://www.drjohnsullivan.com/content/view/81/33/*.

4. Peter Norvig, "Hiring: The Lake Wobegon Strategy," *Offical Google Research Blog*, March 11, 2006, *http://googleresearch.blogspot.com/2006/03/hiring-lake-wobegon-strategy.html*.

5. David A. Vise, *The Google Story* (London: Macmillan, 2005).

6. Greg Linden, "Early Amazon: Interviews," *Geeking with Greg*, February 21, 2006, *http://glinden.blogspot.com/2006/02/early-amazon-interviews.html*.

7. Sara Robinson, "Computer Scientists Optimize Innovative Ad Auction," *SIAM News* 38, no. 3 (April 2005).

8. Kevin J. Delaney, "Google Adjusts Hiring Process as Needs Grow," *Wall Street Journal*, October 23, 2006.

Chapter 5

1. Susan Lammer, ed., *Programmers at Work: Interviews with 19 Programmers Who Shaped the Computer Industry* (Redmond, WA: Microsoft Press, 1986).

2. Mike Pinkerton, "Time for a change," *Sucking Less, On a Budget*, September 7, 2005, *http://weblogs.mozillazine.org/pinkerton/archives/008843.html*.

3. George Akerlof, "Gift Exchange and Efficiency Wage Theory: Four Views," *American Economic Review* 74, no. 2 (May 1984): 79–83.

4. Joseph Weizenbaum, *Computer Power and Human Reason: From Judgment to Calculation* (New York: Penguin Books Ltd., 1984).

5. Fyodor Dostoyevsky, *The Gambler*, 1867.

Chapter 6

1. Fara Warner, "How Google Searches Itself," *Fast Company*, June 2002.

2. Russ Mitchell, "How to Manage Geeks," *Fast Company*, May 1999.

3. Charles de Secondat, Baron de Montesquieu, *The Spirit of Laws* (London: G. Bells & Sons, Ltd., 1914), *http://www.constitution.org/cm/sol.htm*.

Chapter 7

1. Rajshree Agarwal and Michael Gort, "First Mover Advantage and the Speed of Competitive Entry 1887–1986," *Journal of Law and Economics* 44, no. 1 (2001): 161–178.

2. Ben Elgin, "Managing Google's Idea Factory," *BusinessWeek*, October 3, 2005, *http://www.businessweek.com/magazine/content/05_40/b3953093.htm*.

3. Adam Smith, *An Inquiry into the Nature and Causes of the Wealth of Nations* (1776), *http://www.adamsmith.org/smith/won-index.htm*.

4. Paul Graham, "Cities and Ambition," May 2008, *http://www.paulgraham.com/cities.html*.

5. Peter Schwartz and Kevin Kelly, "The Relentless Contrarian," *Wired*, August 1996.

6. William Baumol, *The Free Market Innovation Machine: Analyzing the Growth Miracle of Capitalism* (Princeton, NJ: Princeton University Press, 2002).

Chapter 8

1. Marissa Mayer, interview by Mark Hurst, October 15, 2002, *Good Experience*, *http://goodexperience.com/2002/10/interview-marissa-mayer-produc.php*.

Chapter 9

1. "At Google, Innovation is Not Just Fun, Games," *LA Times*, June 12, 2006.

2. Margaret Bradley, "Gaspard-Clair-François-Marie-Riche de Prony: His Career as Educator and Scientist" (PhD thesis, Coventry Lanchester Polytechnic, 1984).

3. Nelson Schwartz, "Emperor of Steel," *Fortune*, July 2006.

4. Thomas Davenport, "Competing on Analytics," *Harvard Business Review*, January 1, 2006.

5. G. Th. Guilbaud, *Leçons d'à-peu-près* (*Lessons of Approximately*) (Paris: Christian Bourgois, 1985).

6. Laurent Lafforgue, "Mathematics and Truth" (address at reception for Academy of Sciences members accepted in 2003, June 2004).

7. Sergey Brin, James Davis, and Hector Garcia-Molina, "Copy Detection Mechanisms for Digital Documents" (presented at the ACM International Conference on Management of Data (SIGMOD 1995), San Jose, California, May 22–25, 1995).

Chapter 10

1. Ian Hamilton, *The Soul and Body of an Army* (London: Edward Arnold & Co., 1921).

2. John Kenneth Galbraith, *The New Industrial State* (Boston: Houghton Mifflin, 1967).

3. Jeff Bezos, "5 Lessons from Amazon.com's Jeff Bezos," *Wall Street Journal*, February 4, 2000.

4. Robert D. Hof, "Jeff Bezos: 'Blind-alley' Explorer," *BusinessWeek*, August 19, 2004, *http://www.businessweek.com/bwdaily/dnflash/aug2004/nf20040819_7348_db_81.htm*.

5. Uschi Backes-Gellner, Alwine Mohnen, and Arndt Werner, "Team Size and Effort in Start-Up Teams—Another Consequence of Free-Riding and Peer Pressure in Partnerships," University of Zurich, Institute for Strategy and Business Economics (ISU) Working Papers series, March 2004.

6. Rupert Sausgruber, "Testing for TEAM Spirit, an Experimental Study," University of Innsbruck working paper, July 2005.

Chapter 11

1. James D. Thompson, *Organizations in Action: Social Science Bases of Administrative Theory* (New York: McGraw-Hill, 1967).

2. Terry Winograd and Fernando Flores, *Understanding Computers and Cognition: A New Foundation for Design* (Norwood, NJ: Ablex, 1985).

3. Friedrich A. Hayek, *Law, Legislation and Liberty* (Chicago: University of Chicago Press, 1978).

4. Michael Polanyi, *The Logic of Liberty: Reflections and Rejoinders* (Chicago: University of Chicago Press, 1951).

5. Biz Stone, *Who Let the Blogs Out: A Hyperconnected Peek at the World of Weblogs* (New York: St. Martin's Griffin, 2004).

6. Alan Deutschman, "Inside the Mind of Jeff Bezos," *Fast Company*, August 2004.

7. V. A. Graicunas, "Relationship in Organization," *Bulletin of the International Institute Management* 7 (March 1933): 39–42.

8. Douglas Engelbart, "Toward High-Performance Organizations: A Strategic Role for Groupware," in *Groupware '92*, 77–100 (San Francisco: Morgan Kauffman Publishers Inc., 1992).

9. Michael Hammer, "Reengineering Work: Don't Automate, Obliterate," *Harvard Business Review*, July 1, 1990.

Chapter 12

1. Michael Hammer and James Champy, *Reengineering the Corporation: A Manifesto for Business Revolution* (New York: HarperBusiness Essentials, 2003).

2. Jeffrey Dean and Sanjay Ghemawat, "MapReduce: Simplified Data Processing on Large Clusters" (paper presented at the Sixth Symposium on Operating System Design and Implementation, San Francisco, CA, December 6–8, 2004).

3. Sanjay Ghemawat, Howard Gobioff, and Shun-Tak Leung, "The Google File System" (paper presented at the 19th ACM Symposium on Operating Systems Principles, Lake George, NY, October 2003).

Part III

1. Larry Page and Sergey Brin, "The Anatomy of a Large-Scale Hypertextual Web Search Engine," *Computer Networks and ISDN Systems* 30, no. 1–7 (April 1998).

Chapter 13

1. Robert Papper, Michael Holmes, Mark Popovich, Paul Biner, Melinda Messineo, and Mike Bloxham, "The Computer: A Medium for All Reasons," Ball State University Center for Media Design, July 2006.

2. Mark A. Libbert, comment posted on WebmasterWorld.com, July 12, 2006, *http://www.webmasterworld.com/google_adwords/3003366.htm*.

Chapter 14

1. David Court, Thomas D. French, and Trond Riiber Knudsen, "The Proliferation Challenge," *The McKinsey Quarterly*, June 2006, *http://www .mckinseyquarterly.com/Profiting_from_Proliferation_1810*.

2. Everett Rogers, *Diffusion of Innovations* (Glencoe, IL: The Free Press of Glencoe, 1962).

3. Frank M. Bass, "A New Product Growth for Model Consumer Durables," *Management Science* 15, no. 5 (January 1969): 215–227.

4. Frank M. Bass, "A New Product Growth for Model Consumer Durables," *Management Science* 15, no. 5 (January 1969): 217.

5. John Conlisk and Dennis E. Smallwood, "Product Quality in Markets Where Consumers Are Imperfectly Informed," *Quarterly Journal of Economics* 93, no. 1 (February 1979): 1–23.

6. Patrick Grobmann, "In der Zukunft wird Google noch mehr über Sie wissen," *Spiegel Online*, April 3, 2006, *http://www.spiegel.de/netzwelt/ tech/0,1518,409431,00.html*.

7. Andrew McLaughlin, "Google in China," *The Official Google Blog*, January 27, 2006, *http://googleblog.blogspot.com/2006/01/google-in-china.html*.

8. Saul Hansell, "Google Shows New Services in Battle of Search Engines," *The New York Times*, May 11, 2006.

9. Paul Resnick et al., "The Value of Reputation on eBay: A Controlled Experiment," *Experimental Economics* 9, no. 2 (June 2006): 79–101.

10. Doug Edwards, "If a logo changes every day, is it still a logo?" *Xooglers*, May 18, 2006, *http://xooglers.blogspot.com/2006/05/if-logo-changes-every-day-is-it-still.html*.

11. Benedictus de Spinoza, *On the Improvement of the Understanding* (1662), (Whitefish, MT: Kessinger Publishing, 2004).

12. Margaret Blair, quoting Richard Freeman, "Closing the Theory Gap: How the Economic Theory of Property Rights Can Help Bring Stakeholders Back into Theories of the Firm," *Journal of Management and Governance* 9, no. 1 (2005): 33–9.

13. John Gapper, "Search Engines Are Not the Only Sites," *Financial Times*, March 6, 2006.

14. David Kiley, "Advertising Of, By, and For the People," *BusinessWeek*, July 25, 2005, *http://www.businessweek.com/magazine/content/05_30/b3944097.htm*.

Chapter 15

1. Deborah Fallows, "Search Engine Use," Pew Internet & American Life Project, August 6, 2008, *http://www.pewinternet.org/pdfs/PIP_Search_Aug08.pdf*.

2. UK Office for National Statistics, "Internet Retail Sales: December 2008," January 23, 2009, *http://www.statistics.gov.uk/pdfdir/irs0109.pdf*; and "Retail Sales Slow in December," January 28, 2009, *http://www.statistics.gov.uk/cci/nugget.asp?ID=256*.

3. Interbrand, "Best Global Brands: 2008 Rankings," *http://www.interbrand.com/best_global_brands.aspx*.

4. Outsell, Inc., "Outsell, Inc. Pegs Click Fraud as $1.3 Billion Problem that Threatens Business Models of Google, Others," Press Release, July 2006, *http://www.outsellinc.com/site_map/press_releases/click_fraud_threatens_google*; and Click Forensics, "Industry Click Fraud Rate Hovers at 16 Percent for Third Quarter 2008," Press Release, October 23, 2008, *http://www.clickforensics.com/newsroom/press-releases/114-industry-click-fraud-rate-hovers-at-16-percent-for-third-quarter-2008.html*.

5. Alexander Tuzhilin, "The Lane's Gifts vs. Google Report," July 2006, *http://googleblog.blogspot.com/pdf/Tuzhilin_Report.pdf*.

6. George Reyes, quoted by Krysten Crawford, "Google CFO: Fraud a big threat," *CNNMoney.com*, December 2, 2004, *http://money.cnn.com/2004/12/02/technology/google_fraud/index.htm*.

7. Donna Bogatin, "Google CEO on Click Fraud: 'Let It Happen' Is Perfect Economic Solution," *ZDNet*, July 9, 2006, *http://blogs.zdnet.com/micro-markets/?p=219*.

8. Darren Waters, "Google to stay focused on search," *BBC News*, July 3, 2006, *http://news.bbc.co.uk/1/hi/technology/5140066.stm*.

9. Joseph Menn and Chris Gaither, "U.S. Obtains Internet Users' Search Records," *Los Angeles Times*, January 20, 2006, *http://articles.latimes.com/2006/jan/20/business/fi-google20*.

10. James Q. Whitman, "The Two Western Cultures of Privacy: Dignity Versus Liberty," *Yale Law Journal* 113 (April 2004): 1151–1221.

11. Ashlee Vance, "Sun Founders Confess All During Walk Down Workstation Lane," *The Register*, January 12, 2006, *http://www.theregister.co.uk/2006/01/12/sun_founders/*.

12. Hal R. Varian, "Economic Aspects of Personal Privacy," *Privacy and Self-Regulation in the Information Age*, National Telecommunications and Information Administration, June 1997, *http://people.ischool.berkeley.edu/~hal/Papers/privacy/*.

13. Arthur R. Miller, *The Assault on Privacy* (Ann Arbor: University of Michigan Press, 1971).

14. Jessica Litman, "Information Privacy/Information Property," *Stanford Law Review* 52, no. 5 (May 2000): 1283–1313, *http://www-personal.umich.edu/~jdlitman/papers/infoprivacy.pdf*.

15. Susannah Fox, "Online Health Search 2006," Pew Internet & American Life Project, October 29, 2006, *http://www.pewinternet.org/pdfs/PIP_Online_Health_2006.pdf*.

16. Peter Fleischer and Nicole Wong, "Taking Steps to Further Improve Our Privacy Practices," March 14, 2007, *http://googleblog.blogspot.com/2007/03/taking-steps-to-further-improve-our.html*.

17. Luke O'Brien, "Yahoo Betrayed My Husband," *Wired*, March 15, 2007, *http://www.wired.com/politics/onlinerights/news/2007/03/72972*.

18. Matta Security Limited, "Internet-Based Counterintelligence," 2002, *http://www.trustmatta.com/downloads/pdf/Matta_Counterintelligence.pdf*.

19. Online Publishers Association, "Frames of Reference: Online Video Advertising Content and Consumer Behavior," June 2007, *http://www.online-publishers.org/media/file/OPAFramesofReferenceFINA1024.pdf*.

20. Nielsen Online, "Top Online Brands for Streaming Video: October 2008," December 18, 2008, *http://blog.nielsen.com/nielsenwire/online_mobile/top-online-brands-for-streaming-video-october-2008/*.

21. Kevin J. Delaney, "Google Push to Sell Ads on YouTube Hits Snags," *Wall Street Journal*, July 9, 2008, *http://online.wsj.com/article/SB121557163349038289.html*.

22. LiveInternet, "Site Statistics," *http://www.liveinternet.ru/stat/ru/searches .html* (accessed January 26, 2009).

23. Hermann Havermann, quoted in Reuters and ABC Science Online, "Search Engine to Target Arabic Speakers," April 26, 2006, *http://www.abc .net.au/news/newsitems/200604/s1624108.htm*.

24. *People's Daily* online, "Quaero lance un défi à Google," May 11, 2006, *http://french.peopledaily.com.cn/Horizon/4364864.html*.

25. Bill Gates, interview with Peter Jennings, "One-on-One with Bill Gates," *World News Tonight*, ABC, February 16, 2005, *http://abcnews.go.com/wnt/ Story?id=506354&page=2*.

26. Mike Ricciuti, "Microsoft to Google: Hands Off Enterprise Search," *CNET News*, July 13, 2006, *http://news.cnet.com/2100-1012_3-6094002.html*.

27. Eric Schmidt, "A Note to Google Users on Net Neutrality," 2008, *http:// www.google.com/help/netneutrality_letter.html*.

28. Edith Penrose, "Limits to the Growth and Size of Firms," *The American Economic Review* 45, no. 2 (1955): 531–543.

Chapter 16

1. Danny Sullivan, "25 Things I Hate About Google, " March 2006, *http:// blog.searchenginewatch.com/blog/060313-161500*.

2. Albert Hirschman, "Having Opinions, One of the Elements of Well-Being," *American Economic Review* 79, no. 2 (May 1989): 75–9.

3. Friedrich A. Hayek, "The Use of Knowledge in Society," *American Economic Review* 35 no. 4 (September 1945): 519–30.

4. Punt Soni, "Farewell, Google Catalog Search," *Inside Google Book Search*, January 14, 2009, *http://booksearch.blogspot.com/2009/01/farewell-google-catalog-search.html*.

5. Paul A. David, "Clio and the Economics of QWERTY," *American Economic Review* 75, no. 2 (May 1985): 332–7.

6. Sec Form 4, "Insider Stock Transactions–Google, Inc. (GOOG)," *http:// www.secform4/insider-trading/1288776.htm*.

7. Alan D. Jagolinzer, "Do Insiders Trade Strategically Within the SEC Rule 10b5-1 Safe Harbor?" Stanford Graduate School of Business Working Paper, July 2008.

Chapter 17

1. Joseph A. Schumpeter, *Capitalism, Socialism and Democracy* (1942; repr., New York: Harper & Row, 1975), 82–5.

2. U.S. Patent and Trademark Office, "Patent Counts by Class by Year: January 1977–December 2006," *http://www.uspto.gov/go/taf/cbcby.htm*.

3. World Intellectual Property Organization, "World Patent Report: A Statistical Review," *http://www.wipo.int/export/sites/www/ipstats/en/statistics/patents/pdf/wipo_pub_931.pdf*.

4. Klaus K. Brockoff and Alan W. Pearson, "R&D Budgeting Reactions to a Recession," *Management International Review*, October 1998.

5. U.S. Patent and Trademark Office, "Patent Counts by Class by Year: January 1977–December 2006," *http://www.uspto.gov/go/taf/cbcby.htm*.

6. Jason, "What Is The Effect of the "Pending" Recession on Venture Capital Financings of Private Companies?" *Ask the VC*, January 23, 2008, *http://www.askthevc.com/blog/archives/2008/01/what-is-the-eff.php*.

7. Robert G. Picard, "Effects of Recessions on Advertising Expenditures: An Exploratory Study of Economic Downturns in Nine Developed Nations," *Journal of Media Economics* 14, no. 1 (January 2001): 1–14.

8. Ibid.

9. "How Companies Are Marketing Online: A McKinsey Global Survey," *The McKinsey Quarterly*, September 2007, *http://www.mckinseyquarterly.com/How_companies_are_marketing_online_A_McKinsey_Global_Survey_2048*.

10. U.S. Census Bureau, "Online Retail Spending, 2001–2007, and Projections, 2008" *The Statistical Abstract of the United States* (from Jupiter Research, Inc.), *http://www.census.gov/compendia/statab/cats/wholesale_retail_trade/online_retail_sales.html*.

11. DoubleClick Perfomics, "Searcher Moms: A Search Behavior and Usage Study," October 12, 2007, *http://www.performics.com/think-tank/original-research/white-papers/searcher-moms-a-search-behavior-and-usage-study/350*.

12. Arthur M. Okun, *Prices and Quantities: A Macroeconmic Analysis* (Washington, DC: Brookings Institution Press, 1981).

13. Wendy Davis, "Keyword Costs Show Seasonal Spike," *MediaPost*, February 22, 2006, *http://www.mediapost.com/publications/index.cfm?fa=Articles.showArticle&art_aid=40109*.

14. Robert E. Hall, "Recessions as Reorganizations," in *NBER Macroeconomics Annual* (Boston: The MIT Press, 1991).

15. Unsigned review of *Why Wages Don't Fall During a Recession*, by Truman F. Bewley, *The Economist*, February 24, 2000.

INDEX

The Google Way is set in Adobe Garamond Pro. It was printed and bound at Malloy Incorporated in Ann Arbor, Michigan. The paper is 55 lb. Glatfelter Offset B-18, which is certified by the Sustainable Forestry Initiative.